p. 11 Critical thinking requires prior content knowledge.

p 103 Early congressional support for Zionism in Congress to avoid _____ to U.S.
p108: 1967, Zion _____ making
America more libera _____ support for
Israel.

p 134 F: Neo-cons are toxic mix of realism and idealism. = Hobbesian worldview Lockean rhetoric. They are a lobby. They want U.S. to behave like Israel: Use US exceptionalism to justify drive for power.

Foreign Policy, Inc.

Foreign Policy, Inc.

Privatizing America's National Interest

LAWRENCE DAVIDSON

THE UNIVERSITY PRESS OF KENTUCKY

Scholarly publisher for the Commonwealth,
serving Bellarmine University, Berea College, Centre College of Kentucky,
Eastern Kentucky University, The Filson Historical Society, Georgetown
College, Kentucky Historical Society, Kentucky State University,
Morehead State University, Murray State University, Northern Kentucky
University, Transylvania University, University of Kentucky, University of
Louisville, and Western Kentucky University.

Editorial and Sales Offices: The University Press of Kentucky
663 South Limestone Street, Lexington, Kentucky 40508-4008
www.kentuckypress.com

13 12 11 10 09   5 4 3 2 1

Library of Congress Cataloging-in-Publication Data

Davidson, Lawrence, 1945-
  Foreign policy, inc. : privatizing America's national interest / Lawrence Davidson.
      p. cm.
  Includes bibliographical references and index.
  ISBN 978-0-8131-2524-4 (hardcover : alk. paper)
  1. National interest—United States. 2. United States—Foreign relations—
1989- 3. Lobbying—United States. I. Title.
  JZ1480.D383 2009
  327.73—dc22   2008038679

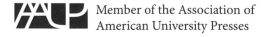 Member of the Association of
American University Presses

This book is dedicated to
Aldous, Afruz, and Sorur

Contents

Acknowledgments

I would like to express my sincere appreciation to Professor Stephen Bronner of Rutgers University. It is with his help that this work moved from its initial presentation as an article entitled "Privatizing Foreign Policy," first published in the Summer 2006 issue of the journal *Middle East Policy,* to its final form in this book. I also would like to express my sincere thanks to Mr. Stephen Wrinn, the director of the University Press of Kentucky. His patience and encouragement assisted me in steadily moving the book toward completion.

Introduction

This book seeks to answer a number of questions:

1. Why do most contemporary Americans pay little attention to issues of foreign policy? Historically, has this always been the case?

2. What are the consequences of this disinterest? For instance, if most Americans are disinterested in foreign affairs, it follows that foreign policy has no necessary connection to popular concerns or even preferences. If this is so, whose concerns and preferences does foreign policy reflect? In other words, where do our foreign policies come from?

3. How do citizens learn what they need to know when suddenly faced with pressing problems of foreign origin? Disinterest in foreign affairs more often than not implies a general ignorance of those affairs. Yet conditions sometimes change, and what we are ignorant of may come to affect our lives. This is certainly the case with foreign policy issues. What are the consequences of ignorance when foreign affairs do impinge on local lives?

4. Most of the lobbies we are familiar with focus on domestic affairs, but are there lobbies that focus on foreign affairs? And, if so, what role do they play in formulating foreign policy? Is there a connection between popular indifference to foreign affairs and the degree of influence that lobby groups exercise on foreign policy?

5. How do our politicians fit into this picture? If most politicians—whether in Congress or the executive branch of government—get elected by a citizenry with little regard for foreign affairs, how much can these elected representatives be expected to know of these matters? Where do they get their information about foreign affairs? Is it just from the State Department? Under such circumstances, how do our elected officials set priorities for foreign policy?

6. Finally, what role does the media in all its different manifestations play in informing a largely ignorant population about foreign affairs? After all, the majority of citizens depend on the media for whatever news they do get about both local and nonlocal events. The difference is that, when it comes to local issues, local people are likely to have some experience by which to judge the accuracy of media reporting. The further from home they go in terms of this reporting, the less local citizens are able to judge objectivity and accuracy. Under such circumstances, just how exposed are local citizens to misinformation and media manipulation?

These are not idle questions. Throughout its history, the United States has entered into hostilities abroad approximately once every thirty years. An enormous amount of the country's resources, both material and in terms of lives, has been devoted to foreign ventures and policies. Yet, as we will see, the average citizen pays little attention to these matters. And, as recent history has shown, these foreign ventures do not always benefit the country. The Vietnam War and the war initiated by the occupation of Iraq were major disasters for the United States and its citizens. Thus, it is important to understand the relation between popular disinterest in foreign affairs and the formulation of policy.

This book explores these questions in terms of both theory and practice. It begins with the laying out of a theory that seeks to explain why, normally, most people are not interested in foreign affairs. This theory centers on the primacy of local space and time in each of our lives. This theory of the natural primacy of localness is a general one. It embraces most Americans most of the time. On the other hand, it is not all-inclusive. Not all people will organize their lives primarily around their local environment and local interests.

There are circumstances that draw relatively small numbers of people to take significant interest in selective matters beyond the local more consistently and persistently than do their neighbors. In the case of foreign affairs, circumstances involving ethnic or religious attachments to foreign places and peoples, as well as economic concerns, can focus attention on matters beyond the local sphere. The same principle can be applied to issues of domestic import. For instance, there are economic issues that may cause businessmen and -women to place a high priority on regional or national issues that affect their livelihood. Gender may also make some people focus on issues of national import, as is the case with women's issues. Even hobbies such as hunting may draw people from diverse locales together on the basis of shared interests.

In exploring the consequences of the minority's more focused interest on nonlocal matters, against the backdrop of general disinterest on the part of the majority, I am led to recognize the major role that interest groups play in the political life of the nation. In doing so, I reconceptualize the nature of American democracy. That is, I challenge the notion that the United States is a democracy of individuals. For, in truth, Americans are not very political beyond their local sphere. The nation's poor voting record at many levels demonstrates this fact. Instead, the United States is, I suggest, a democracy of competing interest groups or lobbies (the minorities mentioned above in their organized forms). In presenting this argument, I introduce the term *factocracy.* This term derives from the Latin root *factio,* which means "faction." In other words, we are, I assert, a nation of competing factions. In effect, naturally occurring localness causes the majority to abrogate political action on nonlocal issues to more motivated minorities—to "factions" that take the form of interest groups or lobbies.

I go on to give both historical and contemporary examples of the impact of lobbies or factions on the nation's foreign conduct. The long-standing influence of economic factions on foreign policy will be examined, as will ethnic and religious lobbies that have also, more recently, become important in this regard. However, I make no attempt to be exhaustive. Not all interest groups are covered, and not all the history and activities of those that are covered are addressed. The aim is to give suggestive evidence for my principle assertions. This book is, if you will, designed to be an extended argument or conversation about a situation that is important to the nation.

The book ends with an example of just how important the issue of factocracy is when it comes to foreign policy. Most Americans, even while bound to their local space and time, assume that the nation has obvious and enduring national interests. However, the logic of the arguments made in this book leads to serious doubts about whether such a thing as national interest really exists. Do the foreign policies pursued by the government in Washington, DC, really benefit the nation as a whole? Or are those policies regularly formulated in such a way as to allow powerful factions to substitute their special interests for national ones?

1

The Popular Disregard
for Foreign Policy

Most Americans do not pay attention to foreign policy issues except when they appear to impinge on their lives. This "out of sight, out of mind" attitude is a function of the fact that, under normal circumstances, a person's consciousness is acculturated to a particular place and time. Localness is, if you will, a natural default position. It dominates consciousness, broadening out only when events originating elsewhere become local themselves. Such impingements from abroad are usually, but not always, seen as negative. Thus, it has most often been at times when foreign threats appear or actually become real—when the Japanese attacked Pearl Harbor, when Soviet missiles were discovered in Cuba, when terrorists collapsed the World Trade Center and rammed the Pentagon—that relatively greater numbers of Americans reluctantly move beyond their local consciousness and show at least temporary interest in events in the wider world or the nation's policies toward the external.[1] More rarely, impositions of foreign origin can be seen by large numbers of citizens as positive or attractive—for example, when the Beatles and the British band craze hit the United States in the 1960s and 1970s, when King Tut's relics toured the country, or when the pope pays a rare visit to the country. However, when the focus on things foreign subsides or periods of apparent threat end, foreign affairs become just that, foreign to the mind of the average citizen, and localism—daily issues specific to an individual's place and time—reasserts its dominance. The Gallup and other polls confirm this situation

5

in terms of foreign relations. Polls taken every presidential election year since 1976 show that, with the exception of 2004 (the first post-9/11 election year), foreign affairs were of little concern to most American citizens.[2] John Mueller, of the Center for the Study of International Peace and Cooperation at the University of Rochester, tells us that "so strong is the evidence on this score that it must be accepted as a fact of life."[3] Therefore, it is not surprising to find that commentators on the public's relation to foreign policy continue to conclude that "the average American is poorly informed on international affairs."[4] Is there anything beyond the default position of localism that causes them to be so poorly informed? Yes. As we will see, for the vast majority whose attention is focused inward, what little they do happen to know of the world beyond America's borders, and the country's foreign relations, is almost invariably what they are told in the mass media. Therefore, one can assume a connection between this source of information and the state of being poorly informed.

That Americans are poorly informed about foreign policy matters does not necessarily mean that they lack opinions on these subjects, or that their opinions will be volatile, or that when viewed as a whole their attitudes will lack coherence. Nor does it mean that, even though their opinions rest largely on an emotive base, they lack the capacity to have an impact on American foreign policy.[5] Americans readily express opinions on foreign affairs *when these matters are brought to their attention.* These opinions can be long lasting and consistent, as seen during the cold war. And, more important, because they most often do not rest on a "fact-checked" evidentiary base, those holding them are susceptible to manipulation in proportion to their overall collective ignorance. That is one of the costs of being poorly informed.

Not normally paying attention to foreign policy also results in an ignorance about, and a disinterest in, how foreign policy is formulated. There are a number of institutions active in American society that try to counteract this ignorance by promoting accurate knowledge on the subject. These include the Choices Program of Brown University, the Web-based information service of the Eric Clearinghouse for the Social Sciences, and the Foreign Policy Association. However, their impact is minimal relative to the size of the population, and, therefore, it is safe to conclude that the great majority of Americans have not had any formal instruction in how foreign policy is *supposed to be arrived at* since what passed for civics in junior high school. Most will not know how foreign policy is made, either in theory or in practice, and probably do not care. If this is, indeed, the case, there would appear to be a certain air of unreality to the statements made by some researchers about the public's relation to American foreign policy. For instance, Glenn Hastedt often refers to the American people as a collective acting to shape foreign policy. He tells us that it is "unclear what goals Americans will want to pursue in their foreign policy" and that it is also "unclear how they will rank threats to the American interest." What is even less clear is whether such statements mean anything in terms of reality. Just who is Hastedt referring to when he writes of "Americans"?[6] Perhaps it is to the relatively small minority of citizens who possess passports[7] or who peruse the scant foreign news that shows up in the American press except in times of war or crisis.[8]

Why Localism Is Natural

Localism is not unusual, particularly in a geographically isolated country like the United States. Under normal conditions, almost all people will naturally focus on their local environment.[9] This is because, on a day-to-day basis, it is our immediate environment that is most important to all of us. The local environment supplies the vast majority with their arena of work and sustenance, and it is where one usually finds one's immediate family circle, friends, and peer groups. It is also where everyday problem solving takes place. To get by, one needs information that allows for this level of problem solving, and that information is to be found only locally. For instance, what matters to most of us on a daily basis are local highway traffic patterns to and from work and school, not air-traffic patterns in and out of the regional airport. On occasion, the latter might concern us, but for most it is only an extraordinary, not ordinary, occurrence. Beyond problem solving, we are interested in the gossip and the comings and goings of our locale just because it is somehow connected to us. Some of us have close relatives or friends abroad, and, in a virtual way, their locale is sometimes integrated with ours, but this too is an exceptional situation. Therefore, rather than events farther off, we are interested in town or neighborhood news: weddings, restaurant and movie reviews, obituaries, local instances of crime, and department store sales. None of this is negated by the advances in communication technology that are said to "epitomize the 'end of geography' and the 'death of distance.'"[10] If we consider the World Wide Web, for instance, we find that, according to a recent Stanford University study, most Americans with access to the Web use it primarily to send and receive personal e-mail and to shop.[11] It would seem that, even in this age of international travel, satellite dishes, and economic globalization, we are still, as individuals and in our daily practice, village oriented.

This situation lends itself to a Darwinian analysis. We know that, in the course of its evolution, the human mind became "equipped with faculties to master the local environment and outwit its denizens."[12] Thus, we all pay most attention to our local environment because it supplies us with the knowledge necessary to make useful and usually successful predictions, secure sustenance, and avoid danger. In other words, a concentration on this arena has survival value. There are nature and nurture components to this process. There are hardwired biological imperatives that make us group oriented, cautious of the unknown, and fear and danger sensitive. This plays itself out most readily in the territorial range in which we dwell. On the other hand, how we manifest these imperatives is a function of what we learn from our personal experiences and the amount and quality of information available to us. As to our immediate daily environment, we can be responsible for gathering the necessary information. Beyond the horizon, however, the issue of information and its reliability lies in the hands of others.

The Perils of Localism

While there are rational reasons for the citizenry to concentrate its interest and knowledge on the near environment, there are also dangers inherent in the fact of localism. "Tuning out the rest of the globe,"[13] as Alkman Granitsas puts it, and concentrating on one's locality means that most of us live largely in ignorance about what is going on beyond the proverbial next hill.[14] This can result in a false sense of security and isolation right up to the moment of crisis when, suddenly it often seems, something threatening looms on the horizon. At that point, the increased numbers of citizens drawn to pay attention to foreign affairs will react on the basis of "the pictures in their heads."

In *Public Opinion,* written back in 1922, Walter Lippman tried to explain the inherent dangers of localism. An important aspect of his critique was the assertion that, the farther from home we look, the more dependent we are on limited and often distorted information coming from sources we know little about. This information underpins "the pictures in their heads"—or "stereotypes" as Lippman characterized them—that flesh out the superficial views we hold of nonlocal events and their possible impact on our lives. Here is how Lippman explained our predicament: "Each of us lives and works on a small part of the earth's surface, moves in a small circle. . . . Inevitably our opinions cover a bigger space, a longer reach of time, a greater number of things, than we can directly observe. They have, therefore, to be pieced together out of what others have reported and what we can imagine."[15]

It is in times of high tension and crisis involving foreign events that we discover our own ignorance of matters that range beyond our local environment. We then turn for information to others who, we assume, know what is going on abroad. What brings us these "experts"—government officials and news pundits (sometimes pejoratively referred to as "talking heads")—is the news media in all its forms. However, as Lippman tells us: "News and truth are not the same thing."[16] One of the reasons for the divergence is the fact that the former is filtered through the minds of the journalist, the news editor, the copyeditor, the headline writer, the producer, the pundit, and so on. And, as the legal theorist Richard Posner tells us, these "experts constitute a distinct class in society, with values and perspectives that differ systematically from those of 'ordinary' people."[17] Yet not many of them are ready to admit that what they present to their locally bound audiences is "in some vital measure constructed out of [their] own stereotypes, according to [their] own code, and by the urgency of [their] own interest."[18] The situation is made worse by the tendency of media outlets, particularly television, to favor experts who are, as Philip Tetlock puts it, "boomsters or doomsters"—that is, pundits who paint overly positive or negative forecasts that hold and increase the audience but whose accuracy, and, therefore, predictive ability, has been shown to be poor.[19]

In other words, both the media providers and the pundits, being as much prisoners of their stereotypes as their viewers and readers are, will have their own pictures in their heads influenced by their own ideologies and vested interests. Those vested interests are often shaped by their personal ideological and political affiliations as well as the media outlets that employ them, and this inevitably leads them to present biased pictures of events from afar (and near ones too—but here the audience may have the necessary direct experience to make a critical and independent judgment). It makes little difference whether some or even most of these media actors and informants truly believe that their positions reflect reality. Consciously or unconsciously, they are in the business of "stylizing" the news.

The problem of stylization is only compounded when we realize that major media outlets—including television stations, cable stations, radio stations, magazine publishers, newspapers, and even motion picture studios—are mostly owned by only a handful of corporate giants such as General Electric, Time Warner, Disney, and Westinghouse.[20] All these large conglomerates are owned and operated by shareholders and executives who have a stake in "establishment politics." A window into the consequences of this situation for media news can be found in the 2007 suit filed by the former anchorman Dan Rather against CBS. In this suit, Rather charges that his former employer, CBS, and its parent company, Viacom, were so closely connected to the Republican administration of George W. Bush that they purposely attempted to suppress, delay, and/or distort negative stories about the Iraq war and administration personnel.[21] Rather's allegations fit well with the position taken by Noam Chomsky and Ed Herman in *Manufacturing Consent*. Here, they put forth a "propaganda model" to describe a mass media that "filters" the news and relies on "information provided by government, business and 'experts' funded and approved by these sources and agents of power."[22] It is such conditions as revealed by Rather and Chomsky and Herman that have now resulted, in the words of Janice Terry, in a "near unanimity of view" on almost all issues, including those having to do with foreign affairs, as well as a tendency for the media to approach the news in a way that is "prone to support the established powerful elite."[23] This is what the retired journalist Andrew R. Cline calls the media's inherent or structural "status quo bias."[24] Such are "the grim realities of modern American journalism" as William Rivers Pitt puts it, that make the old maxim "let the buyer beware" now apply to "the news."[25]

If this process of stylization is consistently applied to events beyond one's "small part of the earth's surface" across the media spectrum and

over a long enough period of time, it will produce generally similar pictures in the heads of local, regional, and even national populations. What
results is a *thought collective*.[26] Thought collectives are artificially created,
communitywide, points of view that take on added strength from the fact
that most people shape their opinions to conform to those of the other
people around them. People want to fit in to their community, and sharing outlooks is an important aspect of this. Once the shared perspective
is in place, there is a natural tendency to reinforce it by seeking out information that supports it. Ultimately, thought collectives can move populations to action on the basis of firmly implanted assumptions that, in turn,
are often based on stereotypes, buzz words, and unanalyzed assertions.

Understanding public perceptions beyond local place and time in the
manner Lippman describes fits well with research on critical thinking.
Daniel Willingham, a professor of psychology at the University of Vir-
ginia, has looked at much of this research and come to the conclusion that
critical thinking is not a skill that can be taught "like riding a bicycle." As
he points out: "The processes of thinking are intertwined with the content
of thought." That is what he calls *domain knowledge*. "Thus, if you remind
a student to 'look at an issue from multiple perspectives' often enough,
he will learn that he ought to do so, but if he doesn't know much about
an issue, he *can't* think about it from multiple perspectives." What are the
consequences of the fact that critical thinking is "dependent on domain
knowledge"? One is that you must have "adequate content knowledge" to
make critical judgments.[27] But adequate content knowledge is just what
the vast majority of citizens do not have about nonlocal events. Superficial
knowledge, such as that gotten from sound bites or brief, one-sided stories,
simply do not supply sufficient knowledge. When we are told that there is
a foreign threat, or when something actually does come over the hill and
thrust itself into our lives, the knowledge we are given by our experts is
almost always insufficient to make an independent and critical judgment,
even if it happens to occur to us that such a judgment is called for.

Take, for instance, the average American's knowledge of such places
as contemporary Cuba or Palestine. If all you know about these places
is what has been laid out to you by cold war or religious stereotypes and
a media very much influenced by ideologically driven groups of Cuban
Americans or Zionists, how do you think critically about what you are
told? How do you even come to the conclusion that there is a need to

✗ SVSU students

consider alternative points of view? Under normal circumstances, most Americans are indifferent to what is happening in Cuba and Palestine and are not going to take the time and trouble to make a study of their history and relationship to the United States. They are going to simply accept the pronouncements of government and media spokesmen as definitive and true.

Objections to this position have been made by researchers who discount the so-called CNN effect—the claim that television and the pictures it can bring into every American's home can, as John Mueller puts it, "set the public's agenda and policy mood."[28] Pointing to the sectarian warfare that brought such horror to Bosnia in the 1990s, such researchers note that media coverage did not spark any public demand for American intervention. But all this tells us is that the media is part of the mix of influences that must come together to place information within a context that appears relevant to the listener's local environment. Bosnia was not presented as a situation relevant to the American observer's local arena. However, if information about a foreign situation is put forth in a multidimensional and coordinated fashion, the media, the pundits, and the government spokesmen all combining to create a consistent and persistent presentation that does relate the events to the audience's locale, the information environment can be manipulated to create the fear and anxiety necessary to move a population to back prepackaged policies. We shall see examples of how this has been done both in this chapter and in chapters 4 and 5.

Therefore, the ways of seeing that result from the formation of a thought collective limit domain knowledge and, thus, narrow the scope of critical discourse. This raises serious questions about the conclusions reached by such investigators as Bruce Berkowitz and James Surowiecki. Berkowitz has made the unsupported claim that Americans are "reluctant to accept 'wisdom' from authority figures."[29] Surowiecki, who has argued for "the wisdom of crowds," tells us: "Even if most of the people within a group are not especially well-informed or rational, it can still reach a collectively wise decision."[30] Yet how can the crowd exercise critical judgment when most or all of its constituent members lack the domain knowledge necessary to be well informed? What is much more probable, particularly in those cases where the situation is presented as relevant to people's lives, is that collective ignorance will lead to something akin to Pavlovian response patterns based on media-conditioned habits of association (Arabs and Muslims are violent, Israelis are just like us, communism is evil, the United States stands for peace, progress, and democracy, etc.). This conclusion would also seem to fit better with research on how the mind structures knowledge. Thus, according to Steven Pinker, the mind uses categories because they allow us to make inferences about the items assigned therein. We do not need to know a lot of details about an object to think we know enough to act/react. All we have to do is know enough to fit it into a category and then infer the rest from the common characteristics of the category in which we have put it. This is a process that facilitates stereotyping.[31] *How the Mind Works*

In times of crisis, most people bound to such stereotyped worldviews will find it almost impossible to think independently, that is, outside their thought collective, about subjects about which they know little but to which they have been sensitized by the media. In a certain sense, the thought collective now takes on the characteristics of a kinship circle. The maintenance of cohesion in the face of outside threats becomes a family affair. As for the minority of skeptics and doubters who somehow escape this acculturation process, most will tend toward silence in the face of community pressure.

The resulting thought collective usually encompasses the political leadership and societal elites as well as the ordinary citizenry. After all, the elites are subject to the same acculturation process and group dynamics as are other groups and are, therefore, in the words of Michael Hunt, "caught up in the web of ideology" that underlies the national self-image.[32] In addition, their uncritical acceptance of the American worldview leads them to protect their assumptions from dissension. In *Victims of Groupthink*, Irving Janis shows how governing political elites create self-reinforcing decisionmaking circles that emphasize the same "glib ideological formulas on which rational policy makers, like many other people who share their nationalistic goals, generally rely in order to maintain self-confidence and cognitive mastery over the complexities of international politics."[33] As it turns out, the decisionmakers who decided on the Bay of Pigs invasion in the early 1960s and led the country into the Vietnam War only a few years later shared the same unquestioned, cold war–generated attitudes about their adversaries as did the general public. In other words, national leaders are no more free of stereotyped pictures

Exceptions where local knowledge contradicts group think: Social Security etc.

of the world than are the masses, despite having available a wider range of information sources. And, as do others, they put a premium on emphasizing attitudes and points of view that affirm group cohesiveness so as to uphold what Earl Ravenal calls "our basic strategic categories—the deep cognitive mind-sets imbedded in our decision-making system."[34] Information or points of view that challenge long-standing assumptions and group unity in the face of real or imagined adversity are filtered out or discounted. And, in the cases cited just above, no elite decisionmaker wished to risk his or her career by taking on the role of devil's advocate.

Thus, just about everyone will come to share, or at least go along with, the range of debate that the "establishment" finds acceptable.[35] It is in this way, among others, that, not just group cohesiveness, but community and national unity is achieved. Therefore, it is not necessary for the manipulation of mass behavior to originate in some conspiratorial cabal standing *outside* the thought collective. Just about everyone—from the national leadership, to the media moguls, to the consumers of news and the voting citizens—is on the *inside* of the prevailing information environment.

Looking at public opinion in this way calls into question the importance of the debate over whether public opinion *should* affect foreign policy. This debate posits two positions. The first position is that of the so-called foreign policy liberals. It holds that an educated public can influence foreign policy in a progressive, humanizing direction. Woodrow Wilson, who rhetorically at least was an advocate of this position, thus argued for "open covenants of peace openly arrived at."[36] That is, he campaigned for foreign policy formulation and international relations carried out in public—without secrecy. This position is based on two assumptions: that the public can be brought to take a serious interest in foreign affairs and that an educated public will always make judgments on foreign policy that will promote peace and international understanding. Elihu Root, secretary of state from 1899 to 1904, put it this way: "The people themselves will have the means to test misinformation and appeals to prejudice and passion based on error."[37]

The second, and opposing, position is that of the so-called foreign policy realists. The realists (with whom Lippman is often identified) assert that foreign affairs is too remote from the citizen's daily life to be of much interest to him or her. However, the realist argument goes further, asserting that, because the crowd is eternally fickle, public influence on

war?

foreign policy would "permit the emotional to govern the rational." As the proponent of realist foreign policy Hans Morgenthau put it: "The rational requirements of a good foreign policy cannot from the outset count upon the support of a public opinion whose preferences are emotional rather than rational."[38]

Both positions award the public and its elites independent status, somehow outside the prevailing thought collective of the community. The liberals assume that education will make the public capable of rendering appropriate judgments regardless of misleading information. But how is such education to be achieved? How is it to escape from the messages that pervade the mass media, creating an information environment that shapes the thought collective? For instance, after World War II, many sociologists and politicians assumed that the American public was returning to a collective attitude of isolationism. Certainly, common sense suggested that a reaction to the horrors of war ought to have moved the public in that direction. But all it took was a few years of fear-producing cold war political pronouncements and parallel news reporting to transform the public into a state of anti-Communist hysteria that produced, by the 1950s, an environment every bit as bad as the Red Scare period following the Russian Revolution. Just so, the realists award a position to officials (including elected officials) making foreign policy that is somehow independent of not only the nation's collective mind-set but also those officials' own private interests (the roots of which are to be found in aspects—whether class or ideology—of the same national community). Thus, the realists say, the nation's leaders will act rationally in terms of foreign policy and be less subject to prejudice and passion than the public. These assumptions are highly dubious. While educated citizens rarely have any effective way of testing information received from the elites and the media, the elites, as Irving Janis points out, are also bound to the attitudes and ideology of the thought collective.[39] This is one of the major reasons why, as Michael Hunt has noted, "policy makers have proven unexpectedly obtuse" to critiques urging fundamental alterations in foreign policy orientations.[40]

Let us take a closer look at the behavior of the politicians, pundits, intellectuals, and government professionals who find themselves in elite positions of foreign policy leadership. They are, according to the realists, the rational element. Yet it comes as no surprise that this group of allegedly dispassionate actors will, on occasion, lie and mislead the public. They almost always do so from within a thought collective paradigm that they share with the public. When the lying is recognized as such, it is usually understood by the liars as a tactical necessity. In other words, it is done because the elites believe that, owing to domestic competitive pressure or deteriorating international conditions, they must use tactics that are unethical or even illegal to manipulate the public for the good of the country. They feel that this is unfortunate, of course, but they see themselves as having good reasons for doing so. These are usually a product of the pictures in their heads that show alleged outside threats that, in turn, necessitate the employment of such tactics. In their minds, they are just trying to promote national interests, which are often seen as identical with the interests of the elites that are framing policy.

Once the lies are decided on and the manipulation of popular opinion begins, the media's role is vital. At this point, there is some risk of running afoul of competing media representing different elements of the business, professional, and bureaucratic elites—each with a range of interpretations of national interests. As we have seen, however, the past thirty years have witnessed a considerable consolidation in the ownership of major media outlets, so, except in extreme cases, the range of views put out by the most powerful and wide-ranging information providers will be relatively uniform. And, in times of crisis, debate is usually reduced to a minimum because it becomes very difficult for the journalists, the producers of news programs, and the newsmagazine and newspaper editors (even those who, ideally, have an investigative approach to news) to make an issue of deceptions and contradictions. Only if and when government policy fails badly will the competitive spirit of the information industry reassert itself and some of the media cease to play the role of accomplice and start to publicly call attention to the lies and contradictions they so readily supported in the recent past.[41]

The Second Gulf War with Iraq as a Case Study

The manipulation of the nation's thought collective by politicians and other elite leaders has always been with us. However, beginning with the era of the Vietnam War, the level of mendaciousness became striking and has often proved deadly on a large scale. Eric Alterman has set out the disastrous consequences of official deception. Three things come through from his study. First, George W. Bush and his associates are presented as the most brazen manipulators to control the executive branch of government in the past hundred years. Certainly, the number of lies issued with straight faces and determined confidence by this administration must qualify for the record books. Second, the most serious lying by presidents is also the most deadly. It entails foreign policy decisions that touch on the waging of war and can result in vast numbers of dead and injured people. And, third, when the media becomes an accomplice in the process of manipulation, whether knowingly or just through uncritical acceptance, the damage is far greater and longer lasting. The lies become extensions of the unexamined assumptions of the pictures in people's heads and can be popularly recognized as lies only when the populace is confronted with catastrophe sufficiently great to bring government and media assertions into open question.[42]

The lying by public officials or their allegedly expert advisers and supporters to a public bound to localism is particularly egregious. The relationship between president and citizen in many ways reflects a sacred trust. Citizens, stuck in their "small part of the earth's surface," are maximally influenced by individuals in whom they have literally *elected* to place their full confidence. In Walter Lippman's day, ordinary citizens had almost no way of verifying the statements issued by their leaders or by a media that translated the events of the world to them. Except for the ever-present small number of skeptics, the only folks who were likely to publicly scoff at the pronouncements of presidents and their representatives were other politicians who wanted to take their place. And, in times of crisis, even they would be muted by patriotic pressures. Today, at the beginning of the twenty-first century, things are, potentially, not quite as bad. Technology—particularly the World Wide Web—gives those who care to use it access to points of view beyond those bound within the parameters of their thought collective. But, as suggested above, its impact is still slight. The number of people who go about searching for alternative points of view on events beyond their local interest is, from the politician's standpoint, statistically insignificant.

A recent example of the consequences of both a population's information dependence and media compliance with official deception can be found in the selling of the disastrous Second Gulf War. Popular acceptance of that war began to evolve when, in his January 29, 2002, State of the Union address, President George W. Bush specified Iraq, along with Iran and North Korea, as part of an "axis of evil." The phrase was, no doubt, meant to be reminiscent of the label given to the alliance between Germany, Italy, and Japan during World War II. The president went on to state: "The United States of America will not permit the world's most dangerous regimes [North Korea, Iran, and Iraq] to threaten us with the world's most destructive weapons."[43] The assumptions presented in the address were that these three regimes were, in fact, "the world's most dangerous," that they possessed "the world's most destructive weapons," and that they were bent on using those weapons (WMDs, or weapons of mass destruction) against the United States.

The vast majority of Americans had no way of knowing whether those assertions were true or false, or something in between. And the media pundits, in this case mostly Tetlock's "doomsters," augmented by editorials and slanted daily reporting, expanded on the president's frightful picture in a distinctly noninvestigative manner.[44] Why investigate when the picture of Iraq as dangerous and evil appeared plausible because twelve years earlier, in August 1990, Iraq had, in fact, acted aggressively by invading Kuwait. This had given rise to the First Gulf War. Iraq's historical claim to Kuwait—admittedly not a sufficient reason for invasion—was unknown to the vast majority of Americans. That factor was part of a picture in the heads, not of Americans, but of Iraqis.

In addition, after the terrorist attacks of September 11, 2001, Americans—who lacked information that would allow them to understand what had happened in an accurate historical context—were collectively sensitized to any possible threats, real or imagined, from the Middle East. And the Bush administration proceeded (erroneously) to implicate the Iraqis in that seminal event. Although Saddam Hussein's regime had not used WMDs in the invasion of Kuwait, it had used chemical weapons (most of which were purchased from the United States) against Iraqi Kurds as well as (with American targeting assistance) Iranian troops during the Iran-Iraq War. Altogether, a stereotyped picture of Iraq as a dangerous and ruthless nation on the verge of possessing nuclear weapons that would most likely be used against the United States and/or Israel was easily painted in the heads of as many as 70 percent of the American people.[45]

Indeed, there are similarities to be found between the selling of the

Bush administration stereotypes and historical descriptions of the spreading of false prophesies about the impending end of the world. Here is one that may be seen as applicable. It is given by Charles Mackay in the classic *Extraordinary Popular Delusions and the Madness of Crowds*:

> A panic terror of the end of the world seized the good people of Leeds and its neighborhood in the year 1806. It arose from the following circumstances. A hen, in a village close by, laid eggs on which were inscribed the words, "Christ is coming." Great numbers visited the spot and examined the wondrous eggs, convinced that the day of judgment was near at hand. . . . Some gentlemen, hearing of the matter, went one fine morning, and caught the poor hen in the act of laying one of her miraculous eggs. They soon ascertained beyond doubt that the egg had been inscribed with some corrosive ink, and cruelly forced up again into the bird's body.[46]

The Bush administration had gone to extreme lengths to produce its own inscribed eggs. Vice President Cheney and Defense Secretary Rumsfeld had bypassed the regular intelligence services and, in October 2001, set up their own in the depths of the Pentagon. It was known as the Office of Special Plans, and its job was to mine the data for scraps of information that might be used to suggest that Iraq had WMDs. Having produced the prophetic eggs in such a fashion, the administration then implanted them, with their doomsday message, within the metaphoric womb of the American media. No "gentlemen" of any influence would admit that the prophesy was contrived until war was well under way and, significantly, had gone from bad to worse.

It is impossible to say with certainty whether President George W. Bush, Vice President Dick Cheney, National Security Adviser Condoleezza Rice, Defense Secretary Donald Rumsfeld, Secretary of State Colin Powell, and their myriad advisers and underlings, not to mention the media pundits contributing to stylizing the news, all truly believed that Iraq had WMDs and that there was a real threat that Saddam Hussein would loose mushroom clouds over America's cities. We do know that many of these people were so determined to convince others that this was the case that they showed aggressive impatience toward those relatively few public skeptics who raised doubts. Any in-house intelligence information that contradicted their assumptions was systematically filtered out or disregarded. As Lippman told us so many years ago: "There is nothing so obdurate to education or criticism as the stereotype. It stamps itself upon the evidence in the very act of securing the evidence."[47] In other words, a group-dynamic process created a very cohesive, overconfident White House decisionmaking team that manifested all the characteristics of groupthink. The deciders became at once perpetrators and victims of their own false worldview. As a result, Janis's description of the groupthink process that attended the Bay of Pigs operation and the escalation in Vietnam perfectly fits the behavior of the Bush administration's inner circle planning the invasion of Iraq: "The concurrence-seeking tendency was manifested by shared illusions and other symptoms. Most crucial were the symptoms that contributed to complacent overconfidence in the face of vague uncertainties and explicit warnings . . . [resulting in] an operation so ill conceived that, among literate people all over the world, . . . the invasion . . . has become the very symbol of perfect failure."[48]

The rapid success in creating in the public mind a stereotyped picture of the threat supposedly posed by Iraq in turn allowed the Bush administration to gain acceptance of a new, publicly declared defense doctrine known as *preemption*. Thus, during a speech at West Point Military Academy in May 2002, the president insisted that America has the right to "strike first" at any enemy that might represent a potential threat: "Our security will require all Americans . . . [to] be ready for preemptive action when necessary to defend our liberty and to defend our lives."[49]

It made no difference that preemption presented as a defense strategy was a contradiction in terms. Nor did the vast majority of Americans immediately demand an analytic look at the evidence that Iraq (much less Iran or North Korea) was an actual threat to their liberty and lives. In fact, it probably never occurred to most of them that such a move was necessary. The administration was presenting apparently convincing evidence. Secretary of State Powell, seen at the time as a person of great integrity, did so quite strikingly during a speech at the United Nations on February 5, 2003. The vast majority of media information sources simply assumed that his presentation was true and reported it immediately. Counterevidence, be it from UN weapons inspectors, academic experts on the Middle East, or antiwar organizations, was downplayed or presented in negative terms. Those offering such counterevidence were dismissed as unreliable, and, perhaps, unpatriotic, witnesses.

It is in this way that manipulated information filled the void of ignorance that Americans had when it came to Iraq. The painted pictures, presented consistently and persistently, created a thought collective and rendered almost natural a procession of events that led to a disastrous and unnecessary war. Later, when troops were committed, men and women had died, and reputations were on the line, even the factual determination, reached officially by the U.S. government by January 2005, that there were no WMDs to be found in Iraq could not stop the process. By that time, the justifications fueling events had shifted from Iraq's alleged threat to the United States to America's holy mission to spread democracy. This was yet another deeply rooted stereotype that was embodied in America's collective self-image. Thus, a stereotypical way of seeing, revolving around claims of mortal threats from abroad, had melded into long-standing assumptions of America's inherent mission to spread its goodness. Both had little basis in reality, yet both had taken on lives of their own within the context of a prevailing thought collective.

That a scenario like this can be played out with such dire and deadly results is, in part, the consequence of a naturally occurring localism. This localism means that, when it comes to foreign policy, most people are bound by a thought collective customized by the mass media. As a result, they are potential victims of a manipulated information environment. That environment can be designed to support policies that soon become resistant to redirection unless they fail in some catastrophic way. It is only at that point that a population (helped along, ironically, by the same media, now reacting to self-evident policy failures) can be brought to question the stereotyped pictures in their heads.

Beneficiaries of Localism

Another consequence of naturally occurring localism and its accompanying disinterest in foreign events is that the general population in effect abdicates influence over policy formulation in favor of whatever numerically small subset of the citizenry does care about foreign affairs. Who these individuals and groups are is determined by many factors. If you are an oil company executive, you will certainly care about U.S. policy toward those areas of the world that have oil reserves. If you are a Cuban living in the United States, you may care very much about U.S. policy toward Castro's Cuba. If you are a Greek American, you might care about Cyprus. Chinese Americans might care about U.S. relations with China or Taiwan. And, of course, most Jewish Americans, along with many Christian fundamentalists, care deeply about America's relations with Israel.

All these groups are the beneficiaries of the phenomenon of localism. For, if the general public does not care about what is happening on the other side of the hill, then, depending on the hill, one or another of these groups will find a relatively clear field for the influencing of policy formulation. If they do so well enough and long enough, it will be their parochial interests that will, eventually, come to define the national interest. It is to how this process occurs within the context of foreign policy formulation that I now turn.

2

Formulating Foreign Policy
in a Factocracy

The problem of public ignorance of and disinterest in the world abroad is compounded by the average citizen's general political apathy. Just as many people are not interested in foreign affairs, many are not, beyond their regional sphere, seriously interested in domestic political affairs either. The further away people go from their home base, the more they feel an ultimate indifference toward political events. This observation is most relevant when times are settled and no collective problems transcending the local are evident. On the other hand, it is certainly true that some people like to discuss politics on a broader level, but such conversations usually end with the shaking of the head or the shrugging of the shoulders. There is a pervasive feeling that one can do about as much about nonlocal politics as one can do about the weather. Thus, the citizens of New Hampshire will show very little interest in a California gubernatorial election (unless one of the candidates is a famous movie star). And, when it comes to national elections, there is an undeniable problem of a pervasive political apathy and alienation reducing the number of citizens who bother to vote. As a consequence, the United States ranks 139th out of 172 democratic countries in voter turnout.[1] This posture of nonparticipation in politics—what Michael Caprini and Scott Keeter call "thin democracy"[2]—only further confirms citizens in their localism. This ubiquitous public orientation means that one must be careful not to exaggerate the meaning of polls purporting to tell us what people think about politics or foreign policy, even when those polls are conducted with statistical so-phistication. There is a difference between answering questions relatively honestly over the phone and believing that the subject matter is impor-tant enough to affect one's daily life.

Once more, feelings of political indifference and alienation are not unusual in a country with a large and complex political system with little or no room for votes of no confidence, third parties, and doable recall efforts. To influence and take advantage of the structures of power, one must be motivated to master the bureaucratic maze and myriad rules of the system. And few are so motivated. As a result, the United States is not primarily a democracy of individuals.

If America's is not a democracy of individuals, what sort of democracy is it? It is, in fact, a democracy of competing interest groups. This too is not unexpected. As Nelson Polsby has observed: "Any political system of much size or scope is likely to contain within it a population sufficiently diverse as to provoke the formation of factions, each pursuing its own interest."[3] The United States is certainly sufficiently diverse for faction for-mation, so I coin a new word to describe the American political system: *factocracy,* deriving from the Latin word *factio* or "faction."

It is doubtful whether America's evolution into a factocracy would have pleased the founding fathers of the country. Many of them were emphatically suspicious of factions. In his Farewell Address, delivered in 1796, George Washington warned that "combinations and associations" could arise that would scheme to "direct, control, counteract, or awe the regular deliberation and action of the constituted authorities" and, thereby, put the desires of a "faction" "in the place of the delegated will of the na-tion."[4] James Madison agreed with Washington on this matter, devoting the whole of the tenth Federalist Paper to the challenge of controlling fac-tions within a republican environment. He defined *faction* as "a number of citizens, whether amounting to a majority or minority of the whole, who are united and actuated by some common impulse or passion, or of interest, adverse to the rights of other citizens, or to the permanent and aggregate interests of the community." It was the claim of majority status that particularly worried Madison. If that claim was made, it became easi-er for "men of factious tempers, of local prejudices, or of sinister designs," "by intrigue, by corruption or by other means," to "betray the interests of the people."[5] In the American system, majority status does not require the backing of a numerical majority of citizens simply because most citizens are not politically engaged. Therefore, Madison's definition can be applied to factions that, in absolute terms, are numerical minorities but, in practicable terms, achieve a level of influence usually reserved for the majority. This scenario fits well the major lobbies that often influence much of U.S. foreign policy.

Madison was of the opinion that "the causes of faction cannot be removed" without destroying the very political liberty he sought to promote. In a collection of notes on the "vices of the political system of the United States," he concluded that it was human nature in the form of the pursuit of self-interest that spurs faction formation. Therefore, all that was left for the makers of the Constitution to do was to create "the means of controlling its effects." In this regard, he accepted David Hume's assertion, made in his essay "On the Idea of a Perfect Commonwealth," that large republics would produce large numbers of factions and, thus, make it harder for any one of them to dominate. In Madison's words: "Society becomes broken into a greater variety of interests, of pursuits, of passions which check each other, while those who may feel a common sentiment have less opportunity of communication and concert."[6] Having convinced himself that the control of factions within a large republic such as the United States was possible, Madison sought that control in the creation of representative bodies with sufficient numbers of delegates to balance and check factionalism. This method of control was to be augmented by constitutional checks and balances between different parts of the government.

Unfortunately, our modern-day situation suggests that Madison's answer may be insufficient to protect what is commonly called the *national interest*. How does our factocracy of competing interest groups really work? Over time, elements of the American population have, for a variety of reasons (having to do most of the time with economics but sometimes with ideology, ethics, ethnicity, race, gender, age, and even shared pastimes), found themselves motivated to political activism. They have come to an understanding of the potential for mastery inherent in the political system and have developed ways around the problem of the powerless, atomized citizen. To do so, individuals with similar interests and goals (those who, according to Madison, "feel a common sentiment") have learned that it is advantageous to come together and form an interest group that pools their financial resources and, if available, their voting numbers. Then, as a lobby, or a faction, they use these resources to influence politicians and government officials, thus shaping legislation and policy to their liking. This happens all the time on the domestic political scene. It also happens on the foreign policy scene. In both cases, it should be noted, the propaganda and rationalizations of a lobby quickly help define the world for its members and equate the group's future well-being with its influence over government policy. In the case of foreign policy formulation, the effectiveness of special interests is helped along by the normal indifference the general public shows toward events abroad. Simply put, the interest group nature of our politics, combined with the consequences of natural localism, maximizes the influence over foreign policy formulation of what George Kennan has called "highly vocal minorities."[7] As we will see, it is in this way that foreign policy becomes *privatized*. To the extent that the power of special interests influences the formulation of foreign policy, the notion that foreign policy is an expression of national interest loses its validity.

Foreign Policy Formulation—the Theory and Its Problems

As with most bureaucratically based processes, there is a formal or theoretical prescription for the formulation of foreign policy, and then there is the real-life way the job gets done. The two do overlap, but all too often the latter takes on a life of its own.

The men who put together the Constitution of the United States had a limited view of the proper range of foreign policy. Indeed, if George Washington's famous Farewell Address is to be taken as representative of the late-eighteenth-century outlook of many of the new nation's leaders, isolationism becomes the country's starting position. As Washington put it: "The great rule of conduct for us in regard to foreign nations is in extending our commercial relations, to have with them as little political connection as possible."[8] The problem, however, was that, in the long run, it proved almost impossible to separate "commercial relations" from "political connection."

For the United States in the late eighteenth century, foreign policy went little beyond making (mostly commercial) treaties, sending out and receiving ambassadors, and protecting overseas trade. There was also, of course, the issue of waging war and making peace, which, in the country's infancy, as often enough in the future, was connected to the issue of trade. Thus, the nation's first postrevolutionary overseas skirmish was with the Barbary pirates, and the War of 1812 was largely motivated, on the American side, by the economic principle of free trade and the related problem of impressment.

When designing the bureaucratic pathways by which foreign policy goals were to be pursued, the founding fathers built into the process their formula for the division of powers. As with so many other aspects of the Constitution, the division of powers was supposed to protect the nation against the authoritarian ways of doing things that the founders associated with the British Crown. The result was a constitutionally prescribed division of responsibilities in foreign policy formulation and execution between the executive branch (the president) and the legislative branch (the Congress) of government.

The division of powers breaks down as follows. The president, as the commander in chief, has constitutional authority to negotiate treaties, send out ambassadors, and run the nation's wars. In carrying out most of these duties, he is to be advised by and work through the Department of State, which, in the words of the Bureau of Public Affairs, is the "lead U.S. foreign affairs agency."[9] Thus, in constitutional terms, the secretary of state is the president's chief foreign policy officer and runs the foreign policy bureaucracy. On the other hand, the Congress has the power to approve all treaties and ambassadorial appointments. Only it can formally declare war. And, just as important, both houses of Congress have budgetary and investigative powers when it comes to foreign affairs.

In theory, the boundaries of responsibility appear clear. The president commands the military, and the Congress declares war. The president negotiates the treaties, and the Senate advises and consents. The president appoints the ambassadors, and the Senate confirms. And so on. However, in practice, things are seldom so neat. Today, policy formulation and execution involves literally thousands of people, both politicians and bureaucrats. Representatives of the two theoretically cooperating branches of government may or may not agree on policy directions and/or emphases. Usually, the Congress will follow the lead of the president, but not always. As one scholar of the process has put it: "While the president is usually in a position to propose, the Senate and the Congress [sic] are often in a technical position to dispose."[10]

Some of the resulting problems and complications are set out by Glenn P. Hastedt in the classic *American Foreign Policy: Past, Present, Future*. For instance, the Senate, which must confirm all treaties by a two-thirds vote, has made changes to 69 percent of the ones brought before it. What this means is that the negotiations carried on with foreign nations by the executive branch of government must of necessity be preliminary in nature. This obviously can frustrate such negotiations and baffle those nations in which executive decisions are not subject to second guesses. The resulting frustration and uncertainty, among other factors, have led the president to assert the right to make "executive agreements" with foreign powers that are not treaties but, according to the U.S. Supreme Court, and also under international law, have the legal force of treaties. This is not a strictly constitutional way of acting, but, in most cases, the legislative branch has gone along with the procedure because, if all international agreements, minor as well as major, were submitted for deliberation and ratification, the Senate would get little other work done. Thus, such executive agreements (sometimes made with prior Senate consent) have become a way of life when it comes to foreign policy. Hastedt tells us: "Between 1946 and 1977 presidents entered into over 7200 executive agreements."[11] Such a great volume precludes the personal involvement of the president in all executive agreements, many of which are concluded by various branches at various levels of the government, such as the State Department and Department of Commerce. It is likely that neither the president nor most members of the Senate even know of the existence of some of these agreements.

These are some of the structural complications flowing from the division of powers. There are other factors complicating the formulation of foreign policy that are not structural yet are quite powerful. For instance, as a U.S. embassy document notes: "The roles and relative influence of the two branches in making foreign policy differ from time to time according to such factors as the personalities of the President and members of Congress and the degree of consensus on policy." To this we may add the role of Kennan's "vocal minorities." That is the reality of a factocracy, particularly on the congressional side of the equation. For instance, it is the dominant position of prevailing interest groups (such as those representing business and labor) that helped influence most of those changes in the 69 percent of treaties mentioned above. In other words, it is often in response to powerful factions or interest groups that Congress and the president will act and react in, as the embassy document puts it, the "ebb and flow of presidential and congressional dominance in making foreign policy."[12]

A Brief History of Foreign Policy in the American Factocracy

Included in the First Amendment to the U.S. Constitution is the rule that Congress "shall make no law . . . abridging . . . the right of the people . . . to petition the government for a redress of grievances." Whether it is reasonable to see the efforts of special interest groups as somehow seeking the "redress of grievances" or not, it is this aspect of the amendment, among other laws,[13] that has opened the door to special interest influence. Nor is this just a recent practice. Indeed, there has never been a time when factions or special interests have not sought to influence the country's foreign policy. As Walter Russell Mead tells us: "Foreign policy and domestic policy are inextricably mixed throughout American history and that means special interests have always been at play in foreign affairs."[14]

Much of this "redress of grievances," as it has affected foreign policy, has been economic in nature.[15] This matches well with the fact that, again from independence on, everyone agreed that economic prosperity was a primary aspect of national interest. The problem was that no one had a strategy to attain uniform prosperity.[16] Therefore, it soon appeared that, if the government catered to the needs of one group (say, East Coast businessmen and the sea-based merchant class), others (say, small agriculturalists) would be subject to economic policies that would hurt them, if only by raising their taxes. This was the sort of situation that helped set Jefferson against Hamilton and contributed to decades of debate over tariffs and land policies.[17] It also spurred the development of the American factocracy.

The Early Emergence of the Factocracy

Thus, for all the founding fathers' aversion to factions, interest group development in relation to foreign policy started early in the young American nation. That meant that James Madison's theory of balance between interest groups was soon sorely tested. The clash of outlooks between Secretary of State Thomas Jefferson and Secretary of the Treasury Alexander Hamilton is a case in point. In the years following the French Revolution, war between England and France grew more likely. It should be remembered that, at this time, the United States was bound to France by a defense treaty signed during the Revolutionary War. Hamilton, who has often been described as one of our country's first foreign policy realists, argued for the abandonment of that treaty and the maintenance of policies that would support trade between the United States and Great Britain. He believed that the future of the nation was tied to a program of commercial development the model for which was England. In this position he was joined by most of the nation's mercantile elite and shipping magnates, most of whom feared above all the economic consequences of a break with England. Hamilton and his mercantile-shipping faction or lobby were willing to sacrifice the interests of other major sections of the nation's economy, such as the agriculturalists, to push their vision of development. Of course, at the time, this position was "realistic" only if one saw as synonymous the rhetoric of the Hamiltonian interest group and a successful program of national development.

Hamilton was opposed by Thomas Jefferson, the so-called idealist in foreign affairs. This idealism was supposed to come, at least in part, from his connecting the honor of the nation with the fulfilling of its treaty responsibilities to the French. However, it is unlikely that Jefferson actually wanted to see the United States embroiled in a European war. He was more inclined toward the country taking a neutral stance. In exchange for neutrality, he would have had the United States demand that England finally fulfill all the requirements of the 1783 Treaty of Paris (which ended the Revolutionary War). This, in turn, would offer some compensation for risking the wrath of France.

Jefferson did not see the nation as fated for the same rapid commercial development as did Hamilton, and he certainly did not believe that trade with Britain was the only key to a prosperous future. His economic roots lay in agriculture. While he was a Southern plantation owner, he was cognizant of the fact that the small farmer was the backbone of the American economy and would remain so for some time yet. He also believed that the American yeoman farmer was a source of the nation's moral fortitude. So, to the extent that Jefferson represented a faction of his own, it was a lobby of agriculturalists who did not want to pay high taxes and otherwise sacrifice for the interests of merchants and shipowners. As one historian has put it, Hamilton's faction may have had a vision of what the nation ought to become, and that allegedly demanded a certain foreign policy orientation, but Jefferson knew what the nation was, and that was the reality to which foreign policy should fit.[18]

In the case at hand, Jefferson sought legislation that would require any neutral stance to reflect "commercial reciprocity, restrictions on foreign commerce to match those placed on American trade and American favors in return for those granted to the United States."[19] This was Jefferson's idealistic position. Ironically, it was that other Southern plantation owner, President George Washington, who sided with Hamilton in the last years of the eighteenth century. Washington went along with the shuffling off of the nation's defensive treaty with France, which hastened hostilities between the two countries. However, his administration did not require anything of Great Britain in return. The British showed no appreciation at all of this act and started seizing American merchant ships trading with France and its colonies. So much for Hamilton's realism.

So here we have an early example of economically driven factionalism that led to the expression of different visions of foreign affairs and different, parochially oriented conceptions of the national interest. The consequences of this went beyond trade policy. The instance described here made it belatedly clear to Madison that it was not just factionalism as it might manifest itself in Congress that had to be worried about. The executive branch of government was also not able to stand above the fray. Even the idolized George Washington was unable to do so. As early as 1794, Madison observed: "The influence of the Executive on events, the use made of them, and the public confidence in the President are an overmatch for all the efforts Republicanism can make."[20] The nineteenth century would confirm the reality of factocracy at *all levels* of the foreign policy formulation process.

Into the Nineteenth Century

In the first half of the nineteenth century, the sea-based merchant traders, particularly those in Massachusetts coastal towns, proved to be effective lobbyists for American naval protection. Their demands were aided by the almost automatic assumption by many revolutionary leaders that American prosperity depended largely on overseas trade. This assumption, and the lobby that encouraged it, spurred the development of the U.S. Navy. It was to protect commerce that the United States fought the Barbary pirates off the coast of North Africa. Most subsequent military actions after this first would be to enhance and/or protect American business interests abroad. Soon after the Barbary affair, the government began providing at least some protection to ships carrying on American trade in the Pacific, which involved, among other commodities, millions of pounds of Chinese tea and Sumatran pepper yearly.

The merchants engaged in this sort of trade often doubled as diplomats or were on intimate terms with such officials. For instance, Condy Raguet served as both the president of the Philadelphia Chamber of Commerce and John Quincy Adams's chargé d'affaires in Brazil, while Charles Biddle served simultaneously as the business agent of the Atlantic and Pacific Transportation Corporation (a company exploring the possibility of an isthmus canal) and Andrew Jackson's government agent in Central America. Sometimes, such merchants literally funded the U.S. government in times of crisis. This was the case when, right after the War of 1812, J. J. Astor loaned the government of James Madison $2.5 million to stave off insolvency. In return, Astor got a commitment from the government to protect his Northwest fur-trading posts as well as the town of Astoria, Oregon, from encroaching British interests. Later, the partnership of William Corcoran and Elisha Riggs (who were not above bribing congressmen for economic favors) would help finance America's expansionist war with Mexico.[21] Once again, the realities of early American politics caused the inextricable mixing of vested (parochial) interests and national interests.

Finally, it should be kept in mind that, through the eighteenth and nineteenth centuries, communication was primitive and the use of newspapers to disseminate information (accurate or otherwise) grew only slowly beyond the larger cities and towns. However, much of the population was rural and farm based and, thus, physically, more isolated than is the case today. Awareness of what was happening beyond one's immediate vicinity was extremely limited and access to information on such matters intermittent at best. Localism contributed to the influence of politically active factional interests.

The Mexican War

During his inaugural address, given on March 4, 1845, James K. Polk, the eleventh president of the United States, said: "The world has nothing to fear from military ambition in our government. While the Chief Magistrate and the popular branch of Congress are elected for short terms by the suffrages of those millions who must in their own persons bear all the burdens and miseries of war, our government can not be otherwise than pacific."[22] A year later, Polk himself would prove this sentiment to be untrue.

On May 11, 1846, Polk delivered a message to Congress that would initiate an American war with Mexico. He did so for economic and strategic reasons as well as an unquestioning faith in Manifest Destiny, the belief that the United States was fated to expand from the Atlantic coast to the Pacific. All the president needed was an excuse to act. It was Texas's rebellion against Mexico and its subsequent desire to join the American Union that would eventually supply the rationale for Polk's expansionist war.

The established border between Mexico proper and the province of Texas was at the Nueces River. When Texas rebelled, it asserted that its border was at the Rio Grande River, which lay further south. When it was granted statehood, the American government took up the Rio Grande border claim. It made no difference to Polk that there was little historical basis for this claim. It would prove a convenient pretext for war with Mexico. What the president would eventually do would be to send General Zachary Taylor with a contingent of troops down to the Rio Grande River and, as the Texan researcher (and CIA officer) John Stockwell later put it, "parade up and down the border—the disputed border—until the Mexicans fired on him."[23] When they finally did so, Polk proceeded to send a war message to Congress in which he claimed that the Mexicans had "invaded our territory and shed American blood on American soil."[24]

Such was the ambition of James Polk. However, in this ambition he was not alone. There were a number of special interest groups that stood to benefit economically from what would be the greatest landgrab in U.S. history (the territory that was eventually annexed covers the present states of California, Nevada, New Mexico, and Utah and a good part of Arizona).

The most important of these groups were Southern politicians and cotton growers. They and their congressional representatives and senators constituted a solid lobby for war with Mexico and the annexation of the northern tier of that country. Their reasons were both economic (the spread of cotton production to new lands) and political (the creation of new slave states). The 1840s was a time of building sectional tension in the United States. The North's growing population had given that region, with its free labor orientation, control of the House of Representatives. However, the Missouri Compromise of 1820 stated that any states created from territories south of the thirty-sixth parallel would allow slavery within their borders. The bulk of the lands that would be taken from Mexico fell into this zone, so the South's commercial and agricultural elite, along with its politicians, pushed hard for a confrontation with Mexico. It should also be remembered that many of the American settlers who had earlier migrated into the Mexican territory of Texas were slaveholders or at least proslavery, and it was they who had mounted the successful revolt that led to Texas independence. Not only did the South's elite hope to see all the territories taken from Mexico become slave states (as it turned out, California, New Mexico, and Utah proved ill suited to the institution of slavery), but it also hoped to divide Texas itself into four separate slave states. This may well have come to pass, thus giving the slavery faction control of both houses of Congress, if the Civil War had not interrupted the process. One irony in all this is that Mexico had outlawed slavery in 1829—a law that the Americans migrating into Texas had ignored—with the result that all the land taken from that country was free territory. It would take American possession to transform it back into slave territory.

Another special interest group that pushed for war was the merchant elite involved in the China trade. Possession of California ports such as those at Los Angeles and San Francisco was of particular importance in this regard because it would cut travel time to the Orient and, thus, help boost American commerce with that part of the world. According to Polk, California's ports would "in a short period become the marts of an extensive and profitable commerce with China and other countries of the East."[25] In 1845, Polk sent John Slidell to Mexico City to try to buy California and New Mexico from the Mexicans. He offered to forgive their $4.5 million debt to the United States and pay an additional $25 million as well. The Mexicans, however, turned the offer down. In fact, they would not even meet with Slidell. War then became the next best option for taking territory the acquisition of which Polk had set as one of the top goals of his administration.

There was also American opposition to Polk's war with Mexico, and, to some extent, this too was economically motivated. Most abolitionists and Northern Whigs opposed the war because they opposed the spread of slavery on principle or feared its consequences for the free labor system. It is also worth noting that some feared that the war would set a bad precedent, it being the result of manipulation and mendaciousness on the part of the president. Thus, shortly before the end of the war, congressmen such as Abraham Lincoln attached an amendment to a bill praising the conduct of General Zachary Taylor (who led U.S. troops into Mexico) criticizing Polk for leading the nation into an unnecessary war. They drew special attention to the way the war had started and implied that the president had lied to the nation about actions allegedly taken by the Mexicans on American soil.[26] In the long run, none of this made any difference.

The Mexican War resulted in a contiguous continental United States that would rapidly fill up with new populations, creating sources of agricultural production and new consumer markets—another added commercial bonus to expansion. Despite the complaints of Polk's political adversaries, many Americans would see the hand of God (Manifest Destiny) behind his policies and the conquests they brought. And, considering that the American God was not only probusiness but also a grand advocate of freedom, the expansion of America would also bring to fruition the great ideals of liberty and democracy. As Walt Whitman put it in 1846, the expansion of the United States meant "the increase of human happiness and liberty."[27] How the great poet reconciled this claim with the South's hoped-for extension of slavery remains a mystery.

As for President Polk himself, he was never in doubt that right was on his and America's side. In his last State of the Union address, delivered on December 5, 1848, he announced: "Peace, plenty and contentment reign throughout our borders, and our beloved country presents a sublime moral spectacle to the world."[28]

On to the Pacific

There was no mystery as to the goals of the entrepreneurs who quickly turned California's ports into jumping-off points for the China trade. Nor did their needs, in terms of their shipping fleets, end on the West Coast. By the mid-nineteenth century, sailing ships were giving way to steam-powered vessels. While such vessels were independent of the vagaries of the wind, they did need coal and coaling stations. It was to arrange access to such strategic coal-bearing points in the Pacific Ocean, as well as to promote greater trade, that Commodore Matthew Perry set off in 1853 to "open" Japan to American influence. Thus, for those Americans influencing foreign policy, Japan was more than a new market in its own right. It was a potential logistic link between the United States and the China trade. This aspect of the expedition came through in the prominent position taken by those clauses of the Treaty of Kanagawa between the United States and Japan—finally signed in March 1858—designating access to coaling facilities for American vessels.[29]

Perry just happened to be a personal extension of the China trade lobby. He was, as one historian puts it, "intimately connected to mercantile families." Indeed, all his closest friends were Americans who were making "fortunes in the China trade" and, therefore, stood to directly benefit from his efforts to open Japan, not only as an American trading partner (optimists of the day were predicting that trade with "Niphon" could amount to $200 million a year), but also as an "outpost" that "lay athwart the major future route to China."[30] Perry's father-in-law was John Slidell (who, as we have seen, had served as James Polk's minister to Mexico), another successful shipping magnate, who helped the young Perry come to understand the navy as "a spearhead of American commerce."[31]

Thus, it seems fitting that the real push for Perry's expedition came from Aaron Haight Palmer, a New York–based businessman and the head of "a lobby for international trade." Palmer had access to both President Millard Fillmore and Secretary of State Daniel Webster. He used this access to urge them to "do whatever it took to establish relations with Japan." When Palmer said that the U.S. government should do "whatever it took," he meant it quite literally. If the Japanese did not comply with American demands for trade access, the use of port facilities, and the establishment of coaling stations (all of which Palmer declared to be a "reasonable" requirement of the "progressive commercial spirit of the age"), the navy should, he felt, commence a "strict blockade of Edo [i.e., Tokyo] Bay."[32] Fillmore and Webster did not go that far. They did, however, agree to grant Perry permission to use defensive force against Japan if necessary.

Perry was a man who believed in his racial and intellectual superiority over the Oriental races. He also believed in a God-given destiny when it came to American expansion across the Pacific. That made God an assumed silent partner of all the other special interests urging on the expedition. When Perry arrived in Japan, these personal assumptions shaped his actions. He quite purposely acted in an aristocratic and disdainful manner. He made many more demands than requests. In fact, he pushed so hard and bluffed so aggressively that it was a wonder he did not provoke an aggressive response to U.S. demands. At that point, of course, he might have had cause to interpret his orders in such a way as to start a war. Still, he knew that there was no need for the United States to invade and take control of Japan, as long as the Japanese did what he wanted. Thus, the goal was not conquest but the imposition of the will of America's controlling commercial factions (put forth as the national will) on Japan.

Backtracking to Hawaii

While Perry set out to open Japan and establish the coal station stepping-stones necessary for the American commercial penetration of China, other Americans had long been at work on the Hawaiian islands. Hawaii had been a way station for New England trading vessels and whalers since the late eighteenth century. In the 1820s, American Protestant missionaries had shown up, and businessmen-planters soon followed. It turned out that Hawaii was a good place to grow sugar-producing crops. Soon, the missionaries and the businessmen teamed up to take over Hawaii in the name of God, civilization, and profit. A combination of the spiritual threat of hellfire and damnation and occasional physical intimidation led one Hawaiian ruler after another to do the bidding of the growing population of foreigners. A good example of this was the infamous "bayonet constitution" of 1887. This constitution, which disenfranchised the poor and empowered the rich while stripping the Hawaiian monarchy of most of its authority, was forced on the reigning king by an American militia group known as the Hawaiian Rifles. Thus, the constitution came into being at the point of a bayonet. Private property rights were introduced, and the planters and merchants who now controlled the economy were granted citizenship. For the Kanaka—the native Hawaiians—it was not God but something quite other that had entered their paradise.

The relentless pressure from outsiders quickly eroded the native culture of Hawaii. The Kanaka, who constituted a shrinking majority, now found themselves, thanks to uncontrolled immigration of both people and diseases such as smallpox from the United States, threatened with the prospect of becoming a minority in their own land. This, of course, engendered resentment and resistance. Both crystallized in January 1891 when a strong-willed and nationalistic new queen came to the throne. This was Lili'uokalani (often known as Queen Lil), who decided that the islands needed a new constitution to restore the rights of the native people.

It is at this point that the historical processes that led to eventual American annexation of Hawaii becomes a tale of two lobbies. The major lobby was the one constituted by the American sugar growers of Hawaii. They were led by Sanford Dole (whose family name still appears on cans of pineapple). Dole and his supporters actually had two problems confronting them. One was that another lobby made up of their business competitors—the sugar growers of Louisiana and Georgia—had managed to have the U.S. Congress institute a tariff law in 1890 that drove up the cost of Hawaiian sugar in the American market.[33] The other was Queen Lil's determination to take back control of the islands.

Learning of Queen Lil's plans, Dole and his supporters formed a conspiratorial group ironically called the Committee of Public Safety. They proceeded to stage a coup and dethrone Queen Lil, who ended up under house arrest. In this act, Dole was aided by the U.S. minister in Hawaii, John L. Stevens. Stevens arranged for 160 marines aboard an American ship at harbor in Honolulu Bay to support the coup. It must be pointed out that Stevens did this on his own and without instructions from his government. It was only after the coup was successful that the minister wired Washington: "The Hawaiian pear is now fully ripe, and this is the golden hour for the United States to pluck it."[34] Simultaneously, Dole sent a formal request for annexation to the government of President Grover Cleveland.

It is uncertain just how much influence the sugar growers of the American South had with Cleveland. Whatever influence was exercised was combined with the president's genuine indignation over the actions taken by the Americans in Hawaii—and particularly Stevens's behavior.

Cleveland concluded: "The military occupation of Honolulu by the United States . . . was wholly without justification."[35] He refused Dole's request for annexation and fired Stevens. However, he did not order the restoration of Queen Lil to her throne, principally because she refused to grant Dole and his supporters amnesty and instead swore to cut off their heads. This was a mistake on her part, for, since she had no further American assistance, Sanford Dole and his clique were able to retain control of the newly declared Republic of Hawaii, from which position they continued their lobbying in Washington for annexation.

Why did Dole, having gained control of Hawaii, still insist on pressing for annexation (while simultaneously insisting that the U.S. government had no right to support Queen Lil because doing so constituted meddling in the affairs of a sovereign nation)? The answer lay in the economics of the sugar industry. The major market for Hawaiian sugar was in the United States. As long as Hawaii was outside the United States, its sugar was subject to the 1890 tariff, which undermined the profits of Dole and his fellow planters. So, if one cannot beat the enemy, one must join them. That was Dole's strategy.

The strategy finally worked when there was a change in leadership and mood in Washington. Cleveland left office in 1897 and was succeeded by William McKinley, who was much more favorable to annexation. The mood changed further when, in 1898, the Spanish-American War broke out. In August of that year, in the frenetic atmosphere of victory over Spain, Hawaii finally became an American territory. Its sugar plantations were soon flourishing once more. In 1900, Dole changed hats and became the territory's first governor. Ex-Queen Lil lived until 1917 and remained the center of a movement to hold onto what native culture was still left.

The Spanish-American War

As noted, it was the fervor generated by the Spanish-American War that eased the way for the annexation of Hawaii. However, this "splendid little war," as Secretary of State John Hay (appointed in August 1898) called it at the time, brought the United States much more territory besides.[36] When the war was finally over, the Americans had taken Guam, the Marianas, Puerto Rico, and the Philippines. Also, Cuba became a U.S. protectorate.

Mainstream historians such as Ralph Raico see this "leap into overseas empire" as a turning point in the foreign policy of the United States.[37] So do revisionist historians like William Appleman Williams.[38] However, as we have seen, the American government had, in general, always been expansionist in policy, and the division of this process into continental and extracontinental activities is an artificial one. Other historians have at least intuited this fact. The most noteworthy one is Frederick Jackson Turner, whose famous frontier thesis was presented in a paper entitled "The Significance of the Frontier in American History" at a session of the American Historical Association in July 1893. The paper, which made Turner's career, postulated that the disappearance of a continental frontier in the 1890s would put in doubt the rugged individualism and republicanism of the American people. This suggested to many at the time that, for the sake of America's national character, the frontier must be transferred overseas and maintained in the form of imperial expansion.

There were also economic arguments for such a program that appeared, at the time, to be very persuasive. One of these arguments, which all imperialist countries asserted, involved the conviction that domestic markets were becoming glutted and would soon be unable to absorb the growing industrial production of their home industries. This feeling was intensified by the periodic placement of tariffs on competing imports, thus closing off selected foreign markets. Here is how Senator Henry Cabot Lodge of Massachusetts expressed this fear—at the same time supplying the remedy, "a foothold in the East"—in a memorandum dated June 6, 1898, to Secretary of State William R. Day:

> We have developed our industries until our home markets can no longer absorb our product. We must have new markets unless we would be visited by declines in wages and by great industrial disturbances, of which signs have not been lacking. The old theory of competing in foreign markets merely by the price of the product is no longer practicable, for . . . under the modern system markets rest on territorial possessions. . . . We occupy toward the East the unrivaled position of holding one side of the Pacific. We cannot hope to get our share of that trade, which, if we take advantage of our opportunities would be the lion's share, unless we have a foothold in the East.[39]

One of the "industrial disturbances" that Lodge must have had in mind was the Panic of 1893 in the United States. Its effects were still felt toward the end of the century. And, although the Panic had its origins in currency policy, many asserted that the cure for the depression it produced lay in a foreign policy of imperialism and the procurement of an ever-greater number of foreign markets.[40] Particularly responsive to this argument were a group of American bankers and politicians that included J. P. Morgan and his associates and William McKinley (soon to be president), Senator Henry Cabot Lodge, Theodore Roosevelt (whom McKinley would make assistant secretary of the navy), John Olney (a Morgan associate and secretary of state from 1895 to 1897),[41] and the aforementioned John Hay. Together, they formed their own faction or interest group pushing a "large policy" that reflected America's alleged destiny to be a great imperial power.[42]

This was the state of affairs prevailing when the U.S. government, and a growing number of media-influenced citizens, took closer notice of an insurrection against Spanish rule that had been going on in Cuba since the 1880s. Around 1895, this insurgency had intensified into a serious war for independence and a ruthless counterinsurgency. This intensification, in turn, produced a series of reactions in the United States, each of which can be tied to an interest group that looked favorably on the prospect of war. These groups were businessmen with investments in Cuba, newspapers that purposely stirred up public excitement for war (yellow journalism) as a marketing technique, and the politicians already predisposed to war and pushing a large policy of foreign expansion. Thus, insofar as the mass media had introduced itself into the picture, the Spanish-American War witnessed some diversification in the type of special interests that sought to influence the formulation of American foreign policy.

Business Groups with Investments in Cuba

According to Grover Cleveland, addressing Congress in 1896, the "actual pecuniary interest" of American citizens in Cuba at this time was "reasonably estimated [to be] at least from $30 million to $50 million." This money was "invested in plantations and railroad, mining, and other business enterprises on the island." The president noted that the amount of American investment was "second only to that of the people and government of Spain." Trade between the United States and Cuba was, by 1894, worth "nearly $96 million" a year.[43]

The most important segment of American investors in Cuba was sugar producers and processors, who, like their Hawaiian counterparts, found that the policies of the local (in this case Cuban/Spanish) government were bad for their business. These included such businessmen as Edwin F. Akins, a good friend of Richard Olney's and a partner in J. P. Morgan and Company. Besides the sugar industry, Americans also had an interest in tobacco, mining, and the carrying trade between Cuba and the United States. Unlike the Americans in Hawaii, those in Cuba were not in a position to engineer a coup. They could only urge Washington to intervene. In a letter signed by some three hundred businessmen and delivered to President McKinley on February 9, 1898, those hurt by the rebellion in Cuba stated that their losses could be estimated at $100 million a year. Given the amount of money at stake, the petitioners asked McKinley to intervene "with the sole object of restoring peace . . . and with it restoring to us a most valuable commercial field."[44] Echoing the circumstances of the Mexican War earlier in the century, these petitioners had allies among other business interests anxious to further penetrate the China trade and/or protect American investments in China in the face of European encroachments.[45] The connection here was the possible seizure of Spanish-held Filipino ports.

Not all members of America's business community desired such intervention. In 1898, the country was just recovering from the depression sparked by the Panic of 1893, and Wall Street stocks went down at the sign of any event that might check that recovery. A war with Spain was, at first, seen as such a possible event. According to the *Commercial and Financial Chronicle* of April 2, 1898: "Every influence has been, and even now is, tending strongly towards a term of decided prosperity, and that the Cuban disturbance, and it alone, has arrested the movement and checked enterprise."[46] Overseas markets were certainly seen as important, but they could be won peaceably, by promoting a worldwide system of free trade. Thus, the Boston stockbroker who explained that "what businessmen really want is peace and quiet" was probably speaking the truth about general attitudes during the first half of 1898.[47] Then, toward the middle of 1898, many in the business community skeptical about intervention in Cuba started to soften their stand, allegedly "on humanitarian grounds."

Antiwar sentiment was completely overcome with news of Dewey's victory at Manila Bay. After that, almost all segments of the business community, in all regions of the country, became imperialistically minded and began insisting that "the Philippines be retained, for the sake of their own trade and as a gateway to Asiatic markets."[48]

Thus, it is probable that the prowar lobbying of some business interests canceled out the antiwar lobbying of other business interests. In other words, if it had been only Americans with investments in Cuba pleading for war, Washington may not have been moved. However, these investors were not alone.

Yellow Journalism

The Spanish American War saw the introduction of an influential and manipulative mass media tactic encouraging, in a propagandistic way, the naturally local U.S. population to take note of foreign events. The tactic is known as *yellow journalism*—using sensationalism, at the expense of facts, to sell papers.[49] The most famous employers of the yellow journalism approach were William Randolph Hearst's *New York Journal* and Joseph Pulitzer's *New York World* (Pulitzer's *San Francisco Examiner* also used the technique). It is the competition between these newspapers for readers that sent journalism standards plunging to a low point not seen since the days of the Alien and Sedition Acts while contributing to public agitation (at least among the papers' readers) for war against Spain.

Both Hearst and Pulitzer used such (for the time) innovative techniques as screaming headlines. For instance, the *New York Journal*'s "Maine Blown Up by Torpedo" announced the news of the explosion that sank the battleship Maine in Havana harbor on February 15, 1898. The headline was based on conjecture rather than evidence. The *Examiner* immediately asked the front-page question: "Did a Spanish Torpedo Do the Awful Work?" When an intercepted letter from the Spanish ambassador in Washington disclosed a less than favorable opinion of President McKinley, the *Examiner* transformed the news into "Spain's Minister Insults the American President," while the *Journal* called it "The Worst Insult to the United States in Its History." Both Hearst and Pulitzer also used sensationalist line drawings such as those of starving Cuban children and Spanish officials strip-searching American women.

Because sensationalism sold papers and also shaped readers' perceptions of events, it has often been asked whether yellow journalism contributed to the pressure for war. The answer is certainly yes, though contributing to the pressure is not the same as being the sole cause. It can be said that tension and a buildup to war were in the interests of publishers who sought to exploit such conditions for the sake of profit. Thus, yellow journalism was a form of war profiteering. This factor is illustrated by the perhaps apocryphal story of an exchange of letters between Hearst and the famous artist Frederic Remington. Hearst had hired Remington to accompany his war correspondent to Cuba in 1897 to supply illustrations for the correspondent's dispatches. As the story goes, Remington found Cuba quite calm and wrote Hearst: "Everything is quiet. There is no trouble. There will be no war. I wish to return." Hearst allegedly replied: "Please remain. You furnish the pictures and I'll furnish the war."[50]

Hearst always denied the story, but the use of yellow journalism has led some historians to conjecture that such a style of reporting increased public pressure for action, which, in turn, increased pressure on Congress, which, in turn, increased pressure on President McKinley, which, in turn, finally brought a declaration of war against Spain.[51] But there are others who are less sure that it was just the newspapers that were manipulating public opinion. They see the drift of public opinion directed by political factions.[52]

Instituting the Large Policy

The so-called large policy was designed to make the industrially maturing, late-nineteenth-century United States a great power on the model of England. This required the United States to become an imperial power with colonies, a large and modern two-ocean navy seeking commercial dominance in Central and South America and, if possible, in the Pacific and Far East as well. As we have seen, this sort of ambition was not new to the last decades of the century. It was a logical extension of the policy positions of the special interests behind the war with Mexico, Perry's mission to Japan, and the annexation of Hawaii.

By the 1890s, the leaders demanding such a large policy included Theodore Roosevelt, the assistant secretary of the navy in the McKinley administration, and Henry Cabot Lodge, then the junior senator from

Massachusetts. They were backed by a number of other members of Congress, mostly from the Northeast and West Coast states, as well as publishers, journalists, academics, and, as we have seen, interested businessmen.[53]

Lodge (a Republican) had lambasted President Grover Cleveland (a Democrat) over the latter's refusal to annex Hawaii in 1893. Indeed, Lodge's criticism of Cleveland's hesitancy to push an internationalist policy would be expressed with the same harshness as his later denunciation of President Woodrow Wilson (also a Democrat) for putting forth an internationalist program following World War I. In any case, in the later 1890s, Lodge's position was that playing an imperialist role on the world stage was the destiny of the United States.[54] Both Lodge and Roosevelt were influenced in this direction by the works of Captain (later Rear Admiral) Alfred Mahan, who had advocated a big navy policy as the key to the nation's commercial success. Mahan believed that, for the United States, a nation that bordered on two oceans, to attain such success, it was necessary to spur production, build a great merchant marine and two-ocean navy, and take colonies.[55] It was Lodge and Mahan together who had, in June 1898, convinced Secretary of State William R. Day to favor the taking of the Philippines.[56]

As for Roosevelt, he was ever anxious for an expansionist and annexationist policy. As soon as he had been appointed assistant secretary of the navy, he wrote Mahan that he was "getting matters in shape on the Pacific Coast." Subsequently, he used his influence to get Commodore Dewey appointed to the command of the Asiatic squadron and "began planning the attack on the Philippines." Indeed, according to Julius Pratt, it was "Roosevelt and Lodge together who prepared the cablegram to Dewey . . . instructing him that in the event of war his duty would be to begin 'offensive operations in the Philippines.' "[57] Roosevelt was also connected to the J. P. Morgan Company, which also saw war with Spain as in its economic interest.[58]

Consequences—Cuba

The combination of special interest lobbying, both directly by concerned business interests and indirectly by yellow journalism, and the preexisting desire of those already in positions of power for a large policy made the outbreak of the Spanish-American War highly probable. And, as was the case with Polk and the war with Mexico, there was plenty of room to doubt the rationales coming from both Washington officials and the press. The war itself lasted only a matter of months in the year 1898. As was usual for wars of that day, more American soldiers died of disease (some 2,000) than of battle wounds (about 385). As for the battles of this war themselves, the United States never lost one. Perhaps that is why Secretary of State Hay thought the whole thing so "splendid."

The island of Cuba was immediately placed under military government. No serious consideration was ever given to the desires of José Martí's revolutionary forces, and they were prevented from entering Havana in any organized fashion. According to Máximo Gómez, one of the rebel generals, this amounted to a betrayal of the Cuban people. Here is part of Gómez's diary entry for January 8, 1899:

> The Americans' military occupation of the country is too high a price to pay for their spontaneous intervention on the war we waged against Spain for freedom and independence. The American government's attitude toward the heroic Cuban people at this history-making time is, in my opinion, one of big business. . . . The transitional government [the U.S. military government] was imposed by force by a foreign power and, therefore, is illegitimate and incompatible with the principles that the entire country has been upholding for so long and in the defense of which half of its sons have given their lives and all its wealth has been consumed.[59]

Gómez was correct that the outlook of the American government had now turned to "big business," which now meant, quite literally, the dividing up of the spoils of war. The American War Department created a committee to oversee what the *New York World* newspaper predicted would be the direction of Cuba's "industrial and commercial future . . . by American enterprise with American Capital."[60] How did this process work?

The new American regime under General Leonard Wood controlled the national budget of Cuba and also had influence over the Cuban banks. Wood's "government" prevented the loaning of money to native landholders for the purposes of farming. The money was used instead to improve roads and sanitation. The consequence was ruinous for the Cubans. The annual loans that farmers had traditionally received were like expected rainfall. When they did not come, seeds could not be purchased, crops could not be sown, and bankruptcy followed. Almost immediately, the representatives of American entrepreneurs such as Andrew W. Preston (a railroad financier) and Henry D. Havemeyer (a sugar planter) appeared in Cuba and bought up the bankrupt property at cheap rates. Simultaneously, the War Department's committee for Cuba dispensed franchises to other American businesses to run Cuba's railroads, electric light company, streetcar company, former Spanish-owned sugar and tobacco plantations, and the like. This all occurred within the first six weeks of occupation.[61]

Eventually, the Platt Amendment, which, among other things, said that U.S. forces could enter Cuba to maintain "a government adequate for the protection of life, liberty, and property," was incorporated into the Cuban constitution (a condition of Washington's withdrawal of its troops from the island). For all intents and purposes, this transformed Cuba into a protectorate of the United States.

Consequences—Philippines

The Cuban revolutionaries did not mount a sustained resistance against the American occupation army. The same cannot be said of the Filipinos, who were led by Emilio Aguinaldo. As soon as they realized that the Americans were determined to replace the Spanish as their colonial masters, they took up arms against the new occupier. This failed war of liberation lasted some three years and claimed as many as 220,000 Filipino lives. Only about 15,000 of those casualties were combatants. The rest were, to use the modern euphemism, collateral damage. Typical of the U.S. military rationale for this anti-insurgency slaughter was that given by one officer: "We must have no scruples about exterminating this other race standing in the way of progress, if it is necessary."[62] The officer offered no accompanying definition of *progress*, but one must assume that he meant a mixture of American colonial rule, free enterprise, and modern technology.

The war to cement the occupation negated the notion of democracy, and the introduction of technology proved a double-edged sword. On the one hand, the Americans did build up-to-date sewage plants and clean water delivery systems. They did improve medical facilities and introduce more enlightened care of the mentally ill. On the other hand, however, there were certain economic problems that came along with agricultural "progress" in the Philippines—problems reminiscent of the situation found earlier in Hawaii. The Philippines was a big producer of sugar. And, as in Hawaii and Cuba, in the Philippines that industry was soon in the hands of American businessmen. What evolved, unfortunately, was an intensified rivalry for a finite market. Sugar producers in the United States (including those in Hawaii) were not in favor of even more competition. Thus, when one former governor general of the Philippines, Dean C. Worcester, said that all the fighting and sorrows of occupation were worth it because, among other things, we had taught the locals how to overcome their "primitive production methods," allowing them to compete on the world market with products like sugar, he earned no friends in Hawaii and the American Deep South.[63]

Finally, did this vicious and quite racist war against the right of Filipino self-determination secure the base for penetration into the China trade that men like Henry Cabot Lodge desired? There seems to be no evidence that it made much impact on U.S. trade with China. Secretary of State Hay issued his famous, if basically ineffective, Open Door notes to the great powers in the fall of 1899. In them, he called for the great powers to publicly pledge to respect China's territorial integrity and assure equal access to trade in their Chinese spheres of influence. The powers evaded the request, and, soon thereafter, Russia took over a good bit of Manchuria, threatening U.S. cotton exports to this part of China. The American position at Manila Bay made no difference. Nonetheless, President McKinley persisted in the myth that taking the Philippines was a wise and seminal act. "I have been criticized a good deal about the Philippines," he said, "but I don't deserve it. The truth is . . . they came to us as a gift from the gods."[64]

Moving into Central America

The Spanish-American War enhanced a strategy of U.S. intervention and subversion, particularly in Central America. This policy was intimately tied to the needs of specific American businesses that not only successfully lobbied the U.S. government for direct assistance when needed but also integrated key American politicians and policymakers into their entrepreneurial structure. The result was accurately described as early as 1907 by Woodrow Wilson when he declared: "Concessions obtained by financiers must be safeguarded by ministers of state, even if the sovereignty of unwilling nations be outraged in the process."[65]

The United States had seen Central and South America as its sphere of influence ever since the declaration of the Monroe Doctrine in 1823. The problem for President Monroe at that time was that the United States did not have the power to enforce his doctrine. But, over the years, that power was developed so that, in 1895, Secretary of State Richard Olney (a Boston lawyer for financial interests tied to J. P. Morgan) could declare: "The United States is practically sovereign on this continent, and its fiat is law upon the subjects to which it confines its interposition."[66] When he said this, Olney was all but threatening war with the British over a border dispute between Venezuela and British Guiana. U.S. mining companies had interests in the goldfields of the disputed territory. By 1898, as we have seen, the United States easily evicted the Spanish from Cuba. In 1903, Teddy Roosevelt's administration was involved in events in Colombia that allowed Colombia's Panama territory to break away and become an independent country. Panama then turned over what would become the Canal Zone to the United States. William Nelson, a J. P. Morgan–connected lobbyist and New York attorney, "literally sat in the White House" helping engineer these events. In the twentieth century, the Monroe Doctrine was still alive, now underpinned by formal treaty structures such as the Inter-American Treaty for Reciprocal Assistance, a 1947 cold war agreement that stated: "An armed attack by any state against an American state shall be considered as an attack against all American states."[67] What was meant by *attack* was kept purposely vague.

As these policy developments proceeded, American economic interests entrenched themselves in Central America. This process was epitomized by the development of the United Fruit Company (UFCO). United Fruit got its start in the 1880s and went through a number of mergers and transformations until today it is known as Chiquita Brands. With the U.S. government as its ally, the company would literally take over the economies, the governments, and the armies of most countries of the region.

Guatemala can be taken as a typical example. United Fruit had moved into the country in the 1890s and, by the mid-1920s, was one of a very few business enterprises that together owned over 90 percent of the country's land. One dictatorship followed another, each making sure that tax laws and employment practices favored the American company. When, finally, in 1954, democracy came to Guatemala in the form of the fairly elected Arbenz government, the result was a mild program of land reform and labor union development. United Fruit executives contacted their Washington allies to seek assistance in removing the offending regime. The response was positive and immediate. Why was this so? James Cockcroft explains it this way: "UFCO's [United Fruit's] law staff and shareholders included many top U.S. government officials. The law office of Secretary of State Dulles had drafted UFCO's 1930 and 1936 agreements with the Guatemalan government. The secretary's brother, CIA Director Allen Dulles, had been a member of UFCO's Board of Directors. The Assistant Secretary of State for Inter-American Affairs, John Moors Cabot, and Cabot's relatives, were UFCO shareholders. Cabot's brother was UFCO president in 1948. Ambassador Henry Cabot Lodge was also a UFCO shareholder. UFCO public relations director Spruille Braden was former U.S. Ambassador to Argentina. . . ."[68]

One reason the U.S. intervention was so effective and immediate was because the Pentagon and the CIA had infiltrated the military establishments of Guatemala and most of the other Central American countries. It should be remembered that these relatively small military establishments were sustained by U.S. aid and trained by U.S. military advisers and that their officers were educated in American war colleges. Thus, by 1954, as Alexander Gray puts it: "The Guatemalan military was more closely aligned with U.S. interests than with the interests of a popularly elected government."[69]

The U.S. military has actively intervened in Central America at least forty times since 1900. By the post–World War II era, it was clear to all that any Central American government that did not subscribe to and maintain "neoliberal" economic policies (i.e., policies that precluded business regulation, anything but the most meager of taxation, land reform, and workers' unions) would be considered Communist and overthrown. Even now, in the post–cold war period, little has changed: witness the 2003 confession of Chiquita Brands officials that the company financed right-wing paramilitary groups in Colombia.[70] In essence, U.S. foreign policy in Central America had long ago been privatized by the economically oriented special interests that represent businesses such as United Fruit/ Chiquita Brands. It is their parochial interests that had come to define the U.S. national interest in this part of the world.

Nor was this pattern confined to the basically agricultural economies of Central America. In his *Open Veins of Latin America,* Eduardo Galeano includes a chapter aptly entitled "The Contemporary Structure of Plunder" to describe the takeover of industry by U.S. corporations backed by the American government and its financial allies such as the International Monetary Fund and the World Bank. Galeano cites the prescient words of Simon Bolivar, who "prophesied shrewdly that the United States was fated by Providence to plague America with woes in the name of liberty."[71] Here, Bolivar foretold two connected developments: the persistent underdevelopment of all of Latin America owing to external control of its economies and the persistent delusion of American citizens that their foreign policies mainly aimed to promote political freedom abroad. The first situation reflected reality; the second, mythology.

Yet the average citizen of the United States paid little or no attention to what his or her government was doing south of the border. A few Americans might vacation on the Mexican Riviera or in the protected enclaves of the Dominican Republic, but they rarely learned about the deep poverty plaguing the region. If, perchance, they happened to glimpse it, they lacked the historical awareness, that is, the "domain knowledge," needed to think critically about it. Few would ever be able to draw a connection between this lack of development and American foreign policy. As a rule, the U.S. mass media told its audience that the government wished only to promote liberal democracy abroad, which, after all, was the politics supporting the economic prosperity of the American middle class. There was an obvious gap between this thought collective position and the history described above. However, localism precluded knowledge of that history, so the media messages and government rhetoric filled the gap, replacing reality with myth.

Conclusion

James Madison's hoped-for balance of forces that would prevent factions from controlling government and its policies never worked. As a consequence, a factocracy manifested itself early on in the nation's political life and also in the process of foreign policy formulation. Throughout most of the nation's formative period, the factions that influenced foreign policy were of an economic nature. They most often identified expansion and trade access to markets as the principle national interests. George Washington conceptualized the national interest so in his Farewell Address when he described the "extending" of "commercial relations" as the nation's foreign policy priority. If there was an ideological underpinning to all this, it was the notion of Manifest Destiny, which supplied rationalizations for expansion that both embraced and went beyond trade and commerce. Thus, the ideological notion of spreading liberty and democracy also became a popular explanation for the direction taken by foreign policy.[72] For the first 120 years or so, this process of expansion confined itself to the North American continent. After 1898, it moved outward into the Pacific and the Caribbean and took on a full-fledged imperialist character. However, any qualitative distinctions made between these two periods are misleading.

When it was occasionally pointed out (as in the case of the Anti-Imperialist League during the Spanish-American War) that imperialist expansion and liberty were at odds, the mass media (with but few exceptions) ignored the claim, which therefore remained a distinct minority position. Some expansionists did respond to the criticism by narrowing the notion of liberty to free trade and the freedom of entrepreneurs to do as they liked, but most, like the media, simply ignored the contradictions all together.

A major reason why this was relatively easy to do was because, as Greg Grandin explains, "by the end of the nineteenth century the idea of 'expansion' enjoyed broad support across the political spectrum, ranging from the financial and manufacturing elites to nationalists, agrarian populists, labor leaders, and secular and Christian reformers."[73] As we have seen, this support had been building throughout much of the nineteenth century. It provided a psychological context that allowed the needs of proexpansion economic factions and lobbies to play key roles in the formulation of American foreign policy. While some diversification in the nature of special interests can be seen in the activities of yellow journalism leading up to the Spanish American War, it was not until the twentieth century that noneconomic special interests—in particular, ethnic and ideological groups—came into their own as factions affecting foreign policy formulation. It is now time to take a look at this development.

3

The Factocracy Diversifies

While economic factions predominated in the first 120 years of America's history, the twentieth century saw the creation of ideologically and ethically based lobbies that demonstrated equal, if not greater, power over the foreign policy formulation process. Here, we must return to the notion of a national thought collective. The reality is that, in the absence of the kind of disaster that undermines collective assumptions, most of the nation's population can be brought by government and media manipulation to see the world in certain ways. During the nineteenth century, the more successful interests aligned their demands with the prevailing ideology of Manifest Destiny and Open Door economics. This transformed national interests into factions' parochial interests and, thereby, made possible the support of populations that were normally little concerned with such matters. In the twentieth century, economic interest groups would stay important, particularly in the case of Central and South America. And, certainly, the economic interests of capitalist society underlay the prevailing ideology of anticommunism. But other factions would now come forward, organized and educated as to the bureaucratic and political ways of foreign policy formulation. Their presence (and sometimes their absence) has helped shape the notion of national interest ever since.

In their introduction to the collection *The Domestic Sources of American Foreign Policy* (which brings together a series of essays touching on the idea of factocracy), Eugene Wittkopf and James McCormick suggest that, since the founding of the nation, those responsible for formulating foreign policy have tied the process to "satisfying the requirements of domestic politics." They go on to assert that, in a "pluralistic" interpretation of foreign policy formulation, where the process is not seen as monopolized by a professional diplomatic bureaucracy, "mass public opinion enjoys greater weight." However, that opinion is "expressed through interest groups."[1]

Tony Smith in his insightful *Foreign Attachments* explains: "The contradictions of pluralist democracy are particularly apparent in the making of foreign policy, where the self-interested demands of a host of domestic actors . . . raise an enduring problem of democratic citizenship: how to balance the rights and interests of the organized few against the rights and interests of the often inattentive many." Smith's focus is largely on the power of ethnic groups, which "seem to place a higher priority on their sense of ethnic identity than on their sense of identity with the greater American community."[2] However, it is not just ethnic groups that play such a role; ideologically driven factions do as well.

In this chapter, I examine a number of lobby groups, both ethnic and ideological, and look at how they have worked to influence foreign policy. In the cases given below, the influence of each group, though strong and effective for a time, eventually fades, owing to either a disastrous failure of the policy the faction advocated or a lack of staying power inherent in the organization. Because of its relevance to the concept of a thought collective, an instance of policy formulation in the absence of lobby influence is also given.

An Ideological Lobby Consistent with the Thought Collective

The most prominent twentieth-century ideological factor shaping the perceptions of Americans in terms of foreign policy has been the cold war paradigm of anticommunism. This paradigm, which was (and, in some cases, still is) the foundation for America's thought collective on capitalist-Communist relations, began to take shape almost immediately after the Russian Revolution in 1917, and its influence proved virulently negative almost immediately. At that time, in the midst of labor unrest, its effects were manifested in Red Scares and the illegal arrest (due process was often suspended) of thousands, and the deportation of hundreds, of immigrants and citizens throughout the United States.[3] Thus, in just a few years, Americans had been brought to a consensus about the Soviet Union and the ideology it represented that was powerful enough to allow elements of the national government to override the nation's own laws.

Of course, the vast majority of Americans had never been to the Soviet Union, never met a Communist, or never even studied these matters in any objective way. Given the reality of localism, they had to rely on newspaper, radio, and government descriptions of what the Soviet Union was like and what communism represented (the case was the same for Soviet citizens when it came to fashioning an idea about the United States and capitalism). Americans were consistently told, in a yellow journalism fashion, that the first was an enemy state and the second an enslaving ideology that was the antithesis of our own allegedly liberating political and economic systems. They were also led to assume that the period of labor unrest that followed World War I, and occasionally resulted in violence, was the result of a left-wing, Communist conspiracy. Anticommunism went latent only as World War II approached and the fascists appeared to be a more immediate danger to friends of the United States such as Great Britain. When, later, Nazi Germany attacked the Soviet Union, the Communists became our unlikely allies. All of a sudden, the totalitarian tyrant Joseph Stalin was "Uncle Joe." Then, after the war, anticommunism reappeared in its cold war form. During the 1950s, the United States went through another virulent Red Scare known as *McCarthyism*.

It was against this historical and psychological backdrop that a number of cold war, anti-Communist lobbies grew up that would help bring the country into one of its most disastrous modern wars—the Vietnam War. One of these groups was the American Friends of Vietnam (AFV), which I use as an example of an organized and ideologically motivated lobby claiming to represent the interests of the majority. As such, the AFV was recruited as a willing ally of the country's national leadership, which held similar ideological views. As an ally of the government, the AFV would encourage and support policy formulation leading the country into war.

In its formative years (1955–1963), the AFV was a remarkably diverse organization, having among its members both conservatives (e.g., Generals John W. O'Daniel and William J. Donovan) and liberals (e.g., the then-senator John F. Kennedy and the American-style democratic socialist Norman Thomas). Liberals and even moderate socialists had long objected to the authoritarian nature of Communist rule. Conservatives were motivated by a militant anticommunism and an unanalyzed assumption that the defeat of the Vietnamese Communists was necessary for the defense of freedom in South Vietnam and Southeast Asia generally. The liberals buttressed their anti-Communist position with "a sympathy for government inspired reform."[4] They, at least, recognized that the South Vietnamese government would have to win the backing of the population if it was to prevail against a Communist movement already admired for defeating French imperialism. Finally, both liberal and conservative members of the AFV believed in the "domino theory." That is, they believed that, if communism were not stopped in South Vietnam, all of Southeast Asia would eventually fall. Neither liberals nor conservatives ever publicly recognized that South Vietnam was an artificial creation of French imperialism or that Ho Chi Minh's political movement represented the nationalist aspirations of most Vietnamese, both North and South.

The AFV leadership was also characterized by an early and strong alliance with the Vietnamese politician Ngo Dinh Diem. Diem has been described as a "fervent" Vietnamese nationalist, "South Vietnam's leading anti-communist," and " 'the only person who has the stature and the authority and the genius' to compete with Ho Chi Minh." Diem was from an upper-class Catholic family and had briefly served as minister of the interior under the French-controlled government of Emperor Bo Dai. In the early 1950s, he came to the United States, where he stayed for two and a half years. During that time, he met an array of influential people, including those who would lead the AFV. Everyone who met him seemed to become convinced that he was the man to transform South Vietnam into a strong anti-Communist state. As Senator Mike Mansfield put it in 1953, Diem "possessed a deep conviction and almost buoyant confidence that he would some day steer his country between colonialism and communism toward freedom."[5] That confidence proved infectious. Certainly, Diem was ambitious. He was also an authoritarian personality and, perhaps, something of a con man. While he successfully convinced most Americans that he favored democracy for Vietnam, he would end up creating a family-based tyranny once he attained power.

For the first fifteen years of its existence, the AFV, functioning as an interest group, was in the enviable position of sharing an anti-Communist ideology not only with the nation's leaders but also with a significant percentage of Americans, who, whether they paid attention to foreign policy or not, were embedded in the information environment of the anti-Communist thought collective. Thus, the organization's influence was not based on economic interests, mobilized ethnic solidarity, or the ability to shape policy by generating votes and campaign contributions. It was based on its assumed ability to effectively promote a shared anti-Communist ideology as it pertained to the defense of South Vietnam.

During the administrations of Dwight Eisenhower and John Kennedy, the AFV used its connections with the media and other private groups to help convince Americans of the necessity of helping Diem achieve power in Vietnam and then continuing to support him in the struggle against the Communists. Given that Diem also had the backing of the U.S. government at this time, the lobby and the government worked as partners in pursuit of the same goals. However, the AFV maintained its support of Diem even as it became (slowly) obvious that he was obsessed with centralizing all power in the hands of himself and his family, blatantly favored the Catholic minority of his country over its Buddhist majority, and was unwilling to institute the necessary social and economic reforms that might win him support in the South.[6] It did so because it saw a Communist takeover of South Vietnam as the likely, and far worse, alternative to the rule of a man it had personal connections to and still hoped to influence. On the other hand, U.S. government officials became disillusioned with Diem more quickly and, in 1963, helped engineer a coup that removed him and his family from power. While shocked by these events and Diem's subsequent assassination, the AFV leadership adapted to the situation and continued to support the series of military juntas that would henceforth rule South Vietnam.

As has been suggested, both American government officials and the AFV leadership worked within an anti-Communist thought collective that upheld the necessity and legitimacy of preventing a Communist government in South Vietnam. In the last half of the 1950s, this led to the unquestioned assumption that, if the North Vietnamese Communists were popular among some groups in the South, it was because the population was being misled or deceived. This assumption was so pervasive that, for the sake of freedom and democracy, the AFV backed the American government's refusal to allow the South's participation in the elections mandated for July 1956 by the 1954 Geneva Accords that ended French domination of Vietnam. As one AFV leader put it: "The spokesmen of American public opinion [the president] should make it clear immediately that the American people will not allow our government to lend a helping hand in the execution of a scheme which will enslave ten million people in the name of a democratic right." It was claimed that the Communist control of the North would not allow for a fair election there. The monitoring arrangements that had been made to assure the elections' fairness were dismissed out of hand. Thus, elections, which most objective observers admitted would be won by Ho Chi Minh even if they were free and fair, could not possibly be allowed. As Senator John F. Kennedy explained, South Vietnam was "the cornerstone of the Free World in Southeast Asia": "Neither the United States nor Free Vietnam [Diem-controlled South Vietnam] is ever going to be party to an election obviously stacked and subverted in advance."[7]

The assumption that one could vote for a Communist government only if one were duped was an axiom of the American thought collective and allowed for such a contradictory stand as refusing monitored elections for the sake of preserving the possibility of democracy. Unfortunately, this same position made war in South Vietnam much more likely. This was so for two reasons. First, the North Vietnamese, denied their chance to come to power democratically, initiated a guerrilla war in the South. Second, American abandonment of the South Vietnamese government became harder as the guerrilla action heated up. Eventually, the various ruling regimes in Saigon proved incapable of rallying South Vietnamese support, and, thus, both the administration of Lyndon Johnson and the AFV came to the conclusion that, if South Vietnam was not to go Communist, there was no alternative to a massive American military buildup there.

In its turn, the American escalation of 1964 and 1965 gave rise to a growing antiwar movement in the United States. This movement functioned as a counterlobby to those interests favoring war. Its growth was helped along by the fact that the Selective Service System, which regularly drafted men into the army, was now greatly expanded. The AFV took it on itself to try to counter the antiwar movement. It produced printed material in support of the war and sought alliances with conservative student groups such as the Young Americans for Freedom. It sent speakers to campuses to aid in opposing student antiwar demonstrations and teach-ins.

As the war went on, it became clear that victory was illusive, and the home front was ever more divided. Yet, in the face of this situation, the AFV stayed consistent in its belief that America's military role in Vietnam was both necessary and moral. So necessary was the AFV's assistance in these troubled years that the Johnson administration went out of its way to help find private financing for the organization.[8] It was not any loss of faith in the war or President Johnson's leadership that finally undercut the Vietnam lobby. It was the slow-motion disaster of defeat that began in January 1968 with the Communist Tet Offensive. It was that countrywide battle that also marked the beginning of the breakdown of the American cold war thought collective as it applied to the struggle in South Vietnam. The war seemed increasingly unwinnable even as more and more Americans were drafted and sent into battle. Under these circumstances, the AFV, along with the U.S. government, was forced onto the defensive by the disaster of a military defeat that could not be hidden from the American people.

When, finally, Richard Nixon's administration began the process of disengagement, the AFV lost its reason for being. The organization's leaders were among the last to concede defeat, and some never did. As late as 1972, AFV leaders were still telling the president of South Vietnam, Nguyen Van Thieu (who had just denounced American negotiations at Paris with the North Vietnamese): "Millions of Americans support your brave stand in defense of your country."[9] It was not until the fall of Saigon to North Vietnamese and Vietcong forces in 1975 that the AFV leaders begrudgingly disbanded the organization.

The AFV was a lobby organization generated out of the ideologically determined thought collective of its time. As long as the anti-Communist consensus underpinning the thought collective stayed stable and strong relative to Vietnam, the AFV stayed influential and a valuable partner of the U.S. government. It was only when that consensus, and, thus, the thought collective itself, started to crumble, owing to wartime stress and ultimate defeat, that the Vietnam lobby declined.

Ethnic Lobbying and the Case of Cyprus

The military disaster in Vietnam caused a momentary questioning of how the United States played out its cold war strategy. This provided a moment when interest groups whose demands were not expressed in terms of the cold war paradigm and even ran counter to it could step forward and have an impact on foreign policy.

A good example of this occurred soon after the American retreat from Vietnam. In the mid-1970s, the country of Turkey, a cold war ally of the United States, invaded and took possession of the northern half of the island country of Cyprus. Cyprus was then an independent state populated by Greeks in the south and Turks in the north. Its government, led at the time by the Greek Orthodox archbishop Makarios, followed a neutral course in the cold war and sought to maintain domestic ethnic peace. However, this latter goal proved unattainable, and, by 1964, there were six thousand UN peacekeeping troops on the island to keep the Greek and Turkish nationalists from each other's throats. In 1974, a coup against Makarios was organized by the rightist military junta then ruling Greece. It was undertaken in part because of the Greek dictatorship's displeasure with the Cypriot government's desire to maintain an independent, binational policy that saw Greeks and Turks as equals. It was that coup, which temporarily displaced Makarios, that triggered the Turkish invasion of northern Cyprus.[10]

For many in the West, the Turkish intercession was as unwelcome as the Greek military's coup. This displeasure was also manifested in the U.S. Congress, which now threatened to cut off American aid to Turkey. This position created serious tension between the legislative branch and the administration of President Gerald Ford. The problem for Ford was that Turkey played an important role as an American cold war ally. There were substantial U.S. military forces in that country, particularly American air force bases and personnel. Of course, the members of Congress knew this to be the case. Thus, one can ask, why was Senate and House displeasure so openly and strongly expressed as to place the Ford administration between Congress's anger with Turkey and the need not to alienate an important ally? Why, in this case, was the anti-Communist thought collective not dictating congressional behavior?

Part of the answer lay in the fact that it was too soon after the debacle of Vietnam (American troops had finally left Vietnam only a year prior) for Congress not to question executive branch foreign policy decisions. As we will see, that same debacle had also temporarily called into doubt the wisdom of strident American anticommunism. Simultaneously, the Greek American community had hastily, though effectively, organized itself to pressure Congress to punish Turkey for its invasion of Cyprus.

Two groups of Greek Americans joined forces for this effort: the American Hellenic Educational Progressive Association and the American Hellenic Institute. Over time, they patterned their activities after those of the American Israel Public Affairs Committee, generating grassroots appeals to Congress for anti-Turkish legislation. This effort was helped along by a publicity campaign partially financed by the Greek embassy in Washington. Of course, neither the Greek Americans nor their supporters in Congress, such as Paul Tsongas of Massachusetts and John Brademas of Indiana, had said much when the Greek junta had tried to destroy the elected government of Cyprus. Brademas even denied that those taking steps against Turkey were supporting a Greek American lobby. Instead, he claimed: "We prefer to think of ourselves as the rule-of-law lobby. . . . We do not feel the U.S. should sanction [Turkish] aggression."[11]

Perhaps as important as the intervention of the Greek American lobby was the fact that there was no effective mobilization of Turkish Americans to deter congressional action against Turkey. Nor did the media, much of which had been temporarily chastened by its prolonged editorial support for the Vietnam disaster, make any consistent effort to back a cold war position that would stress the importance of the Turkish alliance. That meant that the Greek American effort had no real opposition in its attempt to influence Congress.

As a result of a successful lobby campaign put together specifically to get Congress to punish Turkey for its intercession in Cyprus, bills were introduced in both houses to cut off military assistance to Turkey. Turkey, in its turn, threatened to shut down key American bases on its territory if the bills passed. President Ford was now in a bind.

It might be asked at this point where the concept of national interest comes into this story. If one accepted the cold war picture of the world that certainly dominated the outlook of President Ford and his secretary of state, Henry Kissinger, Turkish cooperation was essential to the American national interest because Turkey hosted American bases virtually on the Soviet border. Certainly, it could be argued, those bases—and, thus, Turkey—were more central to the cold war struggle than was northern Cyprus. Certainly, the congressmen threatening to seriously disrupt U.S.-Turkish relations were aware of the cold war. How, then, did they conceptualize the national interest? Or was it possible that no concept of the national interest figured in this case?

President Ford responded to Congress's actions by treating them as a kind of border violation between legislative and executive branch territory. Congress was, he later claimed, meddling "with the President's right to manage foreign policy."[12] Yet, according to the Constitution, Congress was not meddling at all. Its members had every legal right to pass on expenditures such as those that supported U.S. aid to Turkey. Subsequently, Congress actually passed a bill banning arms sales to Turkey. Ford vetoed the bill. Congress then overrode his veto. This tug-of-war between president and Congress (which extended into the Carter administration) was still going when, in 1975, Turkey started restricting U.S. military activities and proceeded to take over twenty-four American bases on its territory. Eventually, in 1978, Congress settled for a compromise bill that allowed aid to Turkey to resume but required the president to report every sixty days on progress (or the lack thereof) toward a resolution of the Cyprus conflict. The hard core allies of the Greek American lobby in Congress decried this compromise as giving in to Turkish blackmail. However, it was probably the case that Greek Americans proved incapable of sustaining an effective lobby effort as it became clear that Turkey would not be swayed by a U.S. arms embargo. Confronted with Turkish stubbornness and the possibility of the permanent loss of valuable military bases, congressmen rediscovered and responded to cold war concerns. To the extent that the Greek American lobby could not continue to present itself as more vital to the reputations and reelection prospects of senators and representatives than could cold war posturing, the resistance to any compromise with the president declined. However, it took almost four years for Congress to arrive at this point.

Repairing the Thought Collective in the Absence of Special Interest Lobbying

The defeat in Vietnam appeared to have consequences other than those manifested in the momentary assertion of the influence of the Greek American lobby. Conservative elements in the United States asserted that the country suffered from a "Vietnam syndrome" because of the way in which the war had ended. That is, the Vietnam experience had created a lack of self-confidence among Americans in their alleged mission to spread and defend freedom in the world and undermined their willingness to sustain the military sacrifices that such a destiny entailed. Conservatives were, therefore, on the alert for opportunities that would allow America to overcome the Vietnam syndrome.

That opportunity seemed to come in 1983 during the administration of Ronald Reagan. On October 24, 1983 (within forty-eight hours of losing 241 marines in the bombing of their Beirut barracks), President Reagan initiated a military invasion of a small Caribbean island called Grenada. The fact that this action was purportedly taken to save the island from communism also helped juxtapose it to the Vietnam syndrome. Here is how the story unfolded. Grenada's prime minister, Maurice Bishop, who had taken power in a popular uprising in March 1979, had turned the island in a socialist direction. He began experimenting with farm cooperatives and was supportive of labor organizations. He instituted free health care and education. Unemployment fell, and literacy went up. More important, from the American point of view, Bishop followed a foreign policy that supported Cuba and the Soviet Union, and he took steps to assure that the island's economy was not dominated by U.S. corporate power. For the U.S. government, successful development following a socialist model was no more welcome in Grenada than it was in Cuba. In an all-too-familiar story, the resulting hostility from the United States caused Bishop to turn to Cuba for economic and military assistance. Then, in October 1983, Bishop's government fell to a coup apparently inspired by ambitious ideologues to Bishop's political left. This coup, which resulted in Bishop's execution, was the excuse for the U.S. invasion.

The invasion got bipartisan support in Congress and across the mainstream media spectrum. Ignoring the fact that the invasion was a clear violation of international law as well as constitutionally questionable, the action turned into a popular precedent for what today we would describe as a "preemptive strike" (to prevent Grenada allegedly falling even more deeply under Communist control) and "regime change." There was also the publicly declared motive to save a small number of American medical students studying on the island from assumed danger. The media delivered the rescue story to the American people without analysis or criticism. The vast majority of Americans had, as usual, no independent way of testing the truth of the government's message or of the supportive statements of various pundits. Public opinion was, thus, predictably favorable. The whole operation was conducted quickly (thus avoiding the invoking of the War Powers Act)[13] and efficiently (thus avoiding too many American casualties). This helped public opinion stay favorable. And, significantly, there was no strong lobby of Americans from, or with specific interest in, Grenada to protest and complain to their representatives and senators as they voted the monies to sustain the operation. In other words, from a political standpoint, the invasion of Grenada offered a near-perfect scenario for legislative-executive cooperation in a foreign policy action as well as giving the conservatives a reason to believe that the Vietnam syndrome was fading. Other such operations would come along, such as the brief but bloody invasion of Panama by the first Bush administration in 1989.

The weakened state of the anti-Communist thought collective arising out of the Vietnam disaster allowed some special interests, such as the ethnically based Greek American lobby, to momentarily influence American foreign policy in ways that appeared to ignore the cold war paradigm. The invasion of Grenada, however, was at least partially designed to overcome the Vietnam syndrome and repair the damage done to the nation's capacity to fulfill its self-proclaimed destiny.

The Vietnam Syndrome and the Neoconservative Lobby

A loosely constructed but enormously influential ideological faction that was and still is motivated to overcome the Vietnam syndrome and return the nation to its place as the leader of the free world is the neoconservative (neocon) lobby.[14] The history of the development of the neoconservative movement can be traced back to the 1930s and the teachings of Reinhold Niebuhr, but, for my purposes, it is sufficient to pick up the story of this evolving interest group with its second generation.[15] At the beginning of the 1970s, the neoconservatives were a group of intellectuals such as William Kristol, John Podhoretz, John Bolton, Paul Wolfowitz, and Jim Woolsey lodged mostly in think tanks such as the American Enterprise Institute and publishing in journals such as *Commentary* and *The Public Interest.* Only a few, like Woolsey, held government positions. The neocons were held together by an overriding anticommunism and a philosophical devotion to the power politics orientation of such political theorists as Leo Strauss and Irving Kristol.[16] As thinkers and critics of foreign policy, the neocons were known to the elites in the State and Defense departments as well as the intelligence agencies (Woolsey was in the

CIA), but they had little or no direct input into the nation's foreign policy. That would soon change. The last twenty years of the century would unexpectedly open up opportunities for them, and they would prove ready, for they were a determined and assertive clique. It was a posture that befit their ancient and macabre vision of the world.[17]

The neoconservative vision of the world was and continues to be one-dimensional and starkly negative. It is, in fact, the right-wing extremist expression of the cold war thought collective. Neocons mix together the Hobbesian and the Manichaean conceptions of reality. The reality pictured by the seventeenth-century political theorist Thomas Hobbes placed mankind in a permanent and hostile state of nature where there is "continual fear and danger of violent death."[18] This perspective was explained for the citizens of the United States by the neoconservative spokesman and author Michael Ledeen, who admonished: "Americans believe that peace is normal, but that is not true. . . . Peace is abnormal."[19]

And what can be said for normality? For the neocons, what is normal is a never-ending war between good and evil that is best characterized by the preaching of the third-century-A.D. religious philosopher Manichaeus.[20] Ledeen spoke for all his associates when he told the BBC: "I know the struggle against evil is going to go on forever."[21] For the neoconservatives, good and evil are absolute in themselves. Each is one-dimensional in its essence, with no room for nuance or subtlety, and both are always clearly recognizable.

Of course, Ledeen and his fellows see themselves as the representatives of good. And they represent good aggressively. Although most of them are "Yankee intellectuals" from the urban centers of America's Northeast, they espouse a "cowboy posture" that requires us all to sleep with our boots on and our guns loaded.[22] After all, evil is always out there.

The operative emotions driving the neoconservatives were, and are, fear and loathing. They feared the revival of Nazi politics and anti-Semitism. They feared the Soviet Union and communism. They feared detente, which they likened to compromising with evil. They feared isolationism. They loathed compromise, which they equated with appeasement. They loathed a liberal approach to foreign policy and its reliance on diplomacy, which they equated with weakness. They loathed the "old Europe." They claimed that they had been "mugged by reality"[23] and, once burnt, were now twice wise.

Why have they, as a special interest group, been led to see the world this way? Some of them have attributed their worldview of fear and loathing to the experiences of relatives who suffered in the Holocaust. According to the neoconservative Richard Perle, the Holocaust was the "defining moment of our history."[24] Here, the evil was easy to identify, and one did not need to spend time examining the source of the problem. The appropriate response, at least in hindsight, was clearly active and aggressive resistance rather than diplomacy and its resulting appeasement. The message taken away from the experience of the Holocaust was that evil must always be resisted with force. The neocons carried this message over in their reaction to the Soviet Union. They indeed saw the Soviet Union as an evil empire, and many of them were paranoid enough to always be seeing Reds under their beds. Despite the fact that it was Nazi Germany that perpetrated the Holocaust, the neocons were soon describing the Soviet Union as the most dangerous empire ever to have existed.[25] It could be dealt with only through the tactics of forceful resistance and not through diplomacy. Hesitation in this regard smacked of appeasement. And, finally, there were others attracted to the neoconservative line who may just have been the type of personality who is always looking for a fight (John Bolton comes to mind). The neocon camp provided them with plenty of opportunities to pick fights.

In any case, this neoconservative world can be interpreted as dangerously oversimplistic. History itself seemed to be all but dismissed by Defense Secretary Donald Rumsfeld with his dubious insight that "stuff happens."[26] As Thomas Wright has put it, what the neoconservatives do is "construct an historical narrative that exclusively associates hawkish positions with success and dovish ones with failure." It should come as no great surprise that such a black-and-white approach has produced very problematic results. As Wright concludes: "Advocating one position as an ideology to inform action across all cases—on the basis that it alone holds the key to success—is a recipe for disaster."[27]

Foreign policy is the passion of contemporary neoconservatives. Having postulated a fear-filled world and dismissed all counterworld-views as naive and dangerous, they advocate a type of foreign policy that flows naturally from their assumptions. The United States requires strong defensive and offensive capabilities because it exists in a world where struggle is the nature of things. The lessons of centuries of experience and effort devoted to the maturation of diplomacy and international law are to be dismissed out of hand on the basis of instances where caution and negotiation proved disastrous. Diplomacy is useful only as a form of delay and deceit.

Toward the end of the cold war, this ideological faction found a home in the administration of Ronald Reagan. The neocons joined the president in celebrating "American exceptionalism." That is, in the style of Manifest Destiny, America was a blessed country called on by God to lead the world. For both Reagan and the neocons, the United States supplied the world with a model for all future societies, both politically, because it embodied democracy, and economically, because it embodied free enterprise. This being so, the hegemony that America was destined to establish around the globe must be a benevolent one. Elliott Abrams, a neoconservative who would get his hands on a bit of power during the Reagan–Bush Sr. era, assured all that the United States is "the greatest force for good among the nations of the Earth."[28]

After the Reagan era, the neoconservatives suffered reverses. They were shunned by the Clinton crowd, and, at the end of the First Gulf War, their advice to immediately bring down Saddam Hussein was not taken by the elder Bush. At that point, they formed the Project for the New American Century, an "educational organization" located in Washington, DC. Its name not withstanding, the organization had as its aim to lobby for a continuation of the neoconservative foreign policy agenda. George Bush Sr. and Bill Clinton may not have been sufficiently responsive to the neocon message, but, with George W. Bush's election in 2000 and the Republican-led Congress that appeared at the same time, new opportunities presented themselves. The neocons found in Bush Jr. and his entourage truly kindred spirits. They were recruited into the government in droves and quickly made alliances with machpolitik advocates such as Defense Secretary Donald Rumsfeld and Vice President Dick Cheney.

The unexpected demise of the Soviet Union had given some of the neoconservatives a period of intellectual anxiety, but they quickly recovered.[29] They soon realized that the absence of the Soviet Union presented a golden opportunity for the establishment of American hegemony. This would have to be done with dispatch, however, because there now existed a power vacuum that, if not rapidly filled by an assertive United States, would allow for the emergence of new challengers, such as China or perhaps even Iran. Knowing this to be so, the neocons solemnly warned that it was time to increase, not decrease, military spending.

This continuing aggressive posture was advocated by the neoconservative Charles Krauthammer, a psychiatrist turned editorial writer on foreign affairs. For Krauthammer, the post–cold war world remained a very dangerous place because advances in technology make peripheral powers and anti-American movements potentially dangerous even to a great power like the United States. As if it were still the cold war, when the Soviet Union was the incarnation of evil, Krauthammer warned of new "embodiments of evil" just on the horizon. After the 9/11 attacks, his message was considered a prophecy come true.[30]

To forestall new challenges and make the world safe for America, Krauthammer and his allies such as Elliott Abrams espoused the need for the United States to "act alone" if necessary to disarm countries and movements that were seen as "upsetting world stability."[31] It would also be necessary to alter the rules of national sovereignty to allow preventive measures to be taken when and where needed. Richard Perle put it this way: "We are going to have to take the war [against the terrorists] often to other people's territory, and all the norms of international order make it difficult to do that. So the president has to reshape fundamental attitudes toward those norms, or we are going to have our hands tied by antiquated institutions [prevailing international law and diplomacy]."[32] This translated into Bush's policies of the preemptive strike and regime change. In a very real way, what the neoconservatives were advocating was expanding the historical approach that the United States had taken toward the nations of Central America and applying it to the world as a whole.

The attacks on the United States that occurred on September 11, 2001, immediately opened the door to a full-fledged neoconservative foreign policy. Soon after the attack, *Newsweek* magazine raised the question: "Why Do They Hate Us?"[33] The pursuit of an answer to that question, in terms of an accurate analysis of American foreign policy in the Middle East since the end of World War II, was quickly suppressed. It was labeled a "blame-the-victim" orientation. In its place came simplistic and nonsensical assertions from politicians and pundits alike—claims such as "they hate our freedoms." As President Bush fashioned the War on Terror, his neoconservative lieutenants began to design a plan to reorganize the Middle East to suit their interpretation of American interests. The subsequent neoconservative-inspired scenario that led to America's 2003 attack on Iraq has been described in chapter 1. Supposedly, this invasion was the first step toward transforming the Middle East into a stable and democratic place.

One might cynically assert that all the talk about promoting democracy that emanated from the Bush White House and its allied neoconservative think tanks (e.g., that they seek to "unleash a democratic cascade" in the Middle East)[34] was only a political cover for the application of "shock and awe." Indeed, making the world safe for both American interests, as defined by the Bush Jr. administration, and democracy has turned out to be a contradictory effort. Thanks to our foreign policy orientation since the end of World War II, democracy, at least in the Middle East and Muslim world, is now most likely to produce anti-American Islamic governments. But, in the world of the neoconservatives, all such complications are made to disappear. After all, if President Bill Clinton can arbitrarily redefine what constitutes sexual relations, President George W. Bush and his neoconservative advisers can redefine what constitutes democracy. In their world, democratic elections must produce pro-American governments (as was expected of mandated elections in Vietnam and later in Latin American countries such as Chile); otherwise, they are a corrupted device of an evil enemy.

This is almost certainly the point of view when it comes to Vice President Richard Cheney, Donald Rumsfeld, Bush's first defense secretary, John Bolton, the former UN ambassador, John D. Negroponte, the former director of national intelligence, and others of the machpolitik persuasion. To this group can be added the Perles, Wolfowitzes, Abramses, and Krauthammers—and President Bush himself. They all seem to truly believe that the mayhem, death, and destruction that they have unleashed on the Middle East will result in a stable, democratic, pro-American region. As the president has repeatedly remarked: "I am confident history will prove the decision we made to be the right decision."[35]

Whatever history might have to say about the matter, we have already considered, in chapter 1, the masterful propaganda campaign that led up to the Second Iraq War. What that campaign did is (using the 9/11 attacks as a jumping-off point) reorient the cold war thought collective from fear of the Soviet Union and communism to fear of the Islamic religion and Muslim fundamentalists. Within the United States, this fear has manifested itself in ongoing attacks against Muslims and those (like Sikhs) who are mistaken for Muslims. These attacks entail arson, assault, slander, and sometimes outright murder. They are paralleled by an extensive form of official ethnic and religious discrimination by local and federal officials, particularly at airports and border crossings. Helped along by popular ignorance of and indifference to foreign policy, Americans have entered on a new cycle of Red (read Muslim) Scares.

Tying Practice to Localness

The buildup and subsequent collapse of support for the Vietnam War, the case of Cyprus, the success of the neoconservative ideology, and the more recent outbreak of anti-Muslim sentiment all suggest that foreign policy can become tied to variants on the theme of localness.

In the case of the Turkish invasion of Cyprus, the anomalous reaction of Congress reflected the structural need of both representatives and senators to reply to effectively pressed constituent demands. James Madison recognized the power of such a local orientation to challenge the national interest. However, he had the idea that designing Congress in a way that spreads representation out over sufficiently large numbers of constituencies, while balancing congressional powers off against the executive branch as well as state legislatures, would reduce the likelihood of powerful locally oriented factionalism. In this way, political room is created for the congressmen and senators to act in the broader interest of the nation as a whole. Yet Madison did not reckon with the inherent apolitical nature of most citizens as a factor that actually can multiply the power of a faction, or a coalition of factions, driven by particular interests but also organized on a national level. Without effective opposition, such factions are unchecked and, therefore, can command the loyalties of Congress across geographic and party lines. Under these circumstances, policy formulation answers to *factio* rather than *demos* (the people, who themselves answer to media manipulation of their information environment), and it is the faction that prevails that can then define national interest in terms of its own needs.

Because localness is characterized by ignorance of and indifference to foreign affairs, it is subject to manipulation by government and organizations that do take an interest in foreign policy and have the ability to influence the media in one direction or another. It is important to remember that, in most cases, a successful faction or lobby, such as the AFV or the neoconservatives, will present its demands in terms that complement the prevailing thought collective. Certainly, that was the case with the AFV as its message took hold simultaneously with a government-inspired media drive to picture South Vietnam as the one place that had to resist communism if the rest of Southeast Asia were to stay free. Quickly, the local populations of America's towns and cities, most of whom did not know where Vietnam was, became believers in something called the *domino theory.* When it came to the neoconservatives and the administration of George W. Bush, the message of the Project for the New American Century became a new rallying point for a reworked national thought collective. "We need," the Project for the New American Century proclaimed, "to accept responsibility for America's unique role in preserving and extending an international order friendly to our security, our prosperity, and our principles"—by adopting an aggressive foreign policy.[36] This is a message not entirely different from its cold war (predetente) predecessor. While it predates the attacks of September 11, 2001, it became the driving force, in the form of the War on Terror, of the U.S. thought collective thanks to that incident. The 9/11 attacks were the archetypical something that comes from over the hill and affects local life.

Whether it is anticommunism or the so-called War on Terror, the media-encouraged themes of the thought collective help define the parameters of local perceptions. Considerations about alleged foreign threats that would never have meant anything in the local worlds of the vast majority of Americans take on exaggerated meaning and, in this state, motivate local people to fear for their future, to go to war, and even to turn on their neighbors. And they will continue to be so motivated right up to the point at which, typically owing to disaster, the media-backed assumptions underlying the thought collective are so shaken that they no longer motivate.

The slow-motion loss in Vietnam is a case in point. It caused a temporary period of popular questioning of the cold war paradigm, which, in turn, caused many Americans to turn away from an aggressive cold war foreign policy in disappointment and disgust. Most reverted to their default position of localness, while some turned to ever more vigorous antiwar protests.

It was shortly after the end of the Vietnam War that the Greek American lobby came on the scene. Greek Americans, like others, are bound to localness, but an ethnic bond causes Greece and Cyprus to be seen as a virtual part of their local world. The Turkish invasion of Cyprus coincided with the momentary breakdown of the cold war paradigm, and, thus, it was at that moment that Greek Americans attained political influence sufficient to cause congressional legislators to act in ways that actually threatened an important cold war alliance.

The fate of the neoconservatives and their power over the prevailing American thought collective will probably be similar to that of the cold warriors following the loss in Vietnam. For an impending loss in the Second Iraq War will cause a backing away from the "muscular foreign policy"[37] that is a product of the neocons' influence. But, alas, as the history laid out in this chapter and the previous one suggests, these periods of paradigm questioning have not proved to last long, nor are they revolutionary.

The workings of the factocracy have shaped American foreign policy again and again. The examples given above involve ideology[38] and ethnic solidarity, and they now join economics as strong driving forces behind faction formation. In 1962, Secretary of State Dean Rusk gave the Senate a document entitled "Instances of the Use of U.S. Armed Forces Abroad, 1789–1945." That document listed 103 operations from the nineteenth and twentieth centuries in which U.S. forces invaded the territory of sovereign states. Rusk was trying to justify America's growing involvement in Vietnam, but the fact was that most of these 103 interventions were carried out to force trade concessions demanded by American business interests and then, subsequently, to protect American lives and property from protesting native elements.[39] Thus were the results of economic-faction-driven foreign policy called on to justify an evolving ideological-faction-driven war. George Washington probably had no inkling that his suggestion that U.S. foreign policy be used for "extending our commercial relations" would be used in this fashion.

What can be concluded from all this is that, in essence, Congress, the political parties, and often the presidency as well do not necessarily act as *national* representative institutions unless the issues before them have a certain neutral quality in relation to organized constituencies and interest groups. But such neutral situations are rare. In the more common case, when factional interests prevail, most politicians will be politically incapable of resisting influential lobby group demands and, correspondingly, incapable of acting in a national way, that is (to hark back to Madison's words), in a way that resists interests "adverse to the rights of other citizens, or to the permanent and aggregate interests of the community." Congress behaves in this nonnational fashion because it is structurally designed to respond to local constituencies. Yet the executive branch of government and the erstwhile national political parties are also not immune from nationally organized, yet sectarian oriented, interest groups. When such groups are powerfully organized, well funded, and *have a staying power that maintains effectiveness for decades on end,* their parochial interests end up defining national interests at all levels of foreign policy formulation. It is to two case studies of this sort that I now turn.

4

Privatizing National Interest—the Cuba Lobby

The characteristics of successful special interests involve excellent organization both in the nation's capital and at the grassroots level, a steady source of revenue, and leadership that is thoroughly versed in the ins and outs of lobbying Congress, the executive branch, and the political parties. Paralleling these attributes, for the exceptionally successful, is a staying power that can last for decades and even generations. Such unique lobbies can truly subvert any notion of national interest so as to make it conform to their parochial interests. One excellent example of this phenomenon is the ongoing influence of the Cuba lobby.

Jorge Mas Canosa and the Creation of Lobby Power

The desires of organized lobbies have often been married to prevailing ideologies. Certainly, the idealization of capitalism by economic special interests and the emotional drive of anticommunism are examples of this phenomenon. However, by the 1990s and the passing away of the Soviet Union, capitalism reigned supreme, and anticommunism could no longer serve to rationalize the identification of an increasingly global corporate capitalism with the national interests of all Americans.

It is against this background that the growth and power of the Cuba lobby must be understood. Cuba had always been presented to the American people as a great danger owing to its Communist status and alliance with the Soviet Union. Occasionally, this picture even approached reality, as in the case of the Cuban Missile Crisis of 1962. But, in the 1990s, not only were the missiles gone, but so too was the Soviet Union. About the same time, the United States began doing brisk business with the residual Communist states of China and Vietnam. Yet Cuba was still presented as a threat to be isolated and undermined. Indeed, as we will see, there would be times when, within the U.S. Congress, the entire trading relationship of the Western world appeared to be held hostage to the issue of Cuba. How could this be so? The answer is that this obviously anachronistic stance was the product of exceptionally successful lobby power.

The Cuba lobby was, primarily, the work of Jorge Mas Canosa. Mas Canosa was born in Santiago de Cuba in 1939. He studied law at the University of Oriente. He took a stand against Castro's turn to the left and went into exile in the United States in 1960. Shortly after arriving in the United States, Mas Canosa joined the Bay of Pigs invasion of his homeland. When that failed, he joined the U.S. Army. Eventually, he became a successful businessman, establishing a telecommunications company known as MasTec that has been valued at $475 million.

But business was not what really drove Mas Canosa. Rather, what drove him was an abiding hatred of Fidel Castro and his government. In 1981, Mas Canosa institutionalized that hatred when he founded the Cuban American National Foundation (CANF). CANF's rapid rise was abetted by Mas Canosa's personality. According to William F. Buckley Jr., while Mas Canosa was a "prickly gentleman," he was also "unrelenting in seeking what he sought" and had a persuasive way of "repeatedly questioning the patriotism of those who disagreed with him and threatened in some cases to ruin their lives or careers."[1] In this unsavory fashion, Mas Canosa quickly became the most influential Cuban American, and his lobby, dedicated to shaping U.S. policy toward Cuba, the second most powerful foreign policy–oriented interest group, in the United States.

American Government Susceptibility to Lobby Power

Mas Canosa and CANF took advantage of the susceptibility of the American government to lobby power. Little else can explain the evolution of American policy toward Cuba as the cold war passed away. Certainly, by the end of the 1980s and the collapse of the Soviet Union, the State

Department and the Pentagon understood that Cuba posed little danger to American interests and policies. For instance, by 1988, Cuban troops were out of Angola and Ethiopia. Soon thereafter, Cuba's direct support for revolutionary movements in Latin and Central America also began to wane. These foreign policy shifts were pragmatic ones forced on the Cuban government as Soviet aid dried up. Without that aid, Havana faced severe economic problems and could no longer afford to assist revolutionary movements worldwide. Its armed forces budget fell, and the number of Cubans under arms was halved.

The Cuban moves brought no reciprocal shift in Washington. Castro had adjusted to international realities, but Washington's reality was of quite a different nature. On the question of Cuba, Washington's reality was and is largely domestic and political. Since Cuban refugees began arriving in the United States, a considerable Cuban American community has grown up in this country. In particular, the states of Florida and New Jersey had seen the growth of politically important Cuban voting constituencies that, as Morris Morley and Chris McGillion observe in their excellent *Unfinished Business,* "no aspirant for local, statewide, or even national office could ignore."[2] This constituency would become the base on which CANF rested.

The model that Mas Canosa used to build his interest group organization was the American Israel Public Affairs Committee (AIPAC). He once commented: "We realized pretty soon that to influence the U.S. political system we must copy . . . the Jewish model, and we became very closely allied with the Jewish lobby and the Jewish movement in Washington." AIPAC was and, as we will see, still is the most powerful lobby affecting foreign policy in Washington and, thus, was a natural source of inspiration for those Cuban Americans who desired to become "player[s] in shaping U.S. policy toward Cuba."[3]

Mas Canosa also played to the tenor of the times. The early 1980s was a period of heightened U.S. intervention in Central America, and CANF soon became allied to the Reagan administration through its public endorsement of American policies in that region. It made little difference to Mas Canosa that these policies supported governments in Honduras, El Salvador, Guatemala, and elsewhere that were often more brutal than Castro's Cuba. This alliance allowed CANF officials access to the White House and to strategically placed members of Congress. Soon, legislation meeting the demands of CANF came rolling out of Congress. For instance, in 1983, only two years after the founding of the interest group, it procured passage of the Radio Broadcasting to Cuba Act, which set up Radio Martí. Mas Canosa soon emerged as the head of the presidential advisory board overseeing the radio station's $12 million annual budget.

CANF also became a direct recipient of U.S. government funds. This was done through regular grants from the National Endowment for Democracy (NED). NED is a U.S. government organization that funnels funds to groups seeking to bring down governments that oppose American policies. These grants are explained as contributions to the promotion of democracy. However, most of the Third World governments that emerge as strong allies of the United States are anything but democratic, and NED gives no money to groups resisting those regimes. Thus, at the very least, NED operates with double standards and, at worst, is a front organization used by the American government to finance selective subversion.

NED was not the only or even the major source of CANF funds. That source was the Cuban American community itself. By 1992, the organization was well funded enough to contribute over $670,000 to the campaign coffers of congressmen and senators of both parties.[4] This demonstration of financial power, combined with the increasingly organized voting power of the Cuban American community, brought the cooperation of key politicians such as Claiborne Pell of Rhode Island, then the chairman of the Senate Foreign Relations Committee, and Robert Torricelli of New Jersey, the chairman of the House Foreign Affairs Subcommittee on the Western Hemisphere.

Some Consequences Relative to National Interests

The economic problems in Cuba in the latter half of the 1980s only encouraged CANF and its government allies to increase pressure on the Castro regime, with the hope that it would soon collapse. For CANF, only the demise of the Cuban regime would do. Any aid going to ordinary citizens of that country must be stopped, and those suggesting negotiations were portrayed as "surrogates of Fidel Castro."[5] This position was successfully communicated to allies in Congress as well as to the Bush Sr. White House, and, as a consequence, the rapidly improving relationship between the United States and Gorbachev's Soviet Union was held hostage to Mas Canosa's desire to utterly wreck Castro and his regime. He and CANF had taken a position that there should be no aid to the Soviet Union as long as it provided aid to Cuba. Soon, Secretary of State James Baker was explaining that the United States was to adopt a "Chinese water torture" approach to Soviet-Cuban relations. "We'll just keep telling them over and over—drop, drop, drop—that they have got to be part of the solution in Central America, or else they'll find lots of other problems harder to deal with." Subsequently, in a meeting with Gorbachev, Bush announced that the Soviet-Cuban link and its consequences in the Americas represented the "single most disruptive element" in U.S.-Soviet relations.[6] If the Soviets wanted agricultural credits from the United States, President Bush observed, they would have to stop putting money into Cuba.[7] This position would become a precedent on which CANF's congressional allies would build, thus eventually causing complications, not only with a decommunizing Soviet Union, but with European allies as well.

It is to be noted that, by taking up the CANF position of no negotiations at a point at which the United States had considerable leverage over an economically weakened Castro government, American politicians not only complicated what can be assumed to have been an important national interest in the transformation of the Soviet Union but also harmed their own potential allies within Cuba. The position of dissidents and reformers in Cuba, as well as of more moderate Cuban American organizations such as the Cuban American Committee for Family Rights, was that the United States should lift the embargo on the island and cease to threaten the Castro government. This policy, they suggested, would create a political environment in Cuba favorable to reform.[8] The Bush Sr. administration never gave these suggestions serious consideration, and its ambassador to the UN Human Rights Commission, Amando Valladares (who had spent twenty-two years as a political prisoner in Cuba), described Cuban dissidents who suggested that the United States open talks with the Castro government as guilty of "treason."[9] Essentially, the Bush Sr. administration decided to sacrifice the interests of the dissidents within Cuba in order to assure themselves of the political benefits of supporting the interests of Mas Canosa and CANF.

Washington also chose to make relations with Havana a point of contention with countries in Latin America so as to stay on the good side of the Cuba lobby. Thus, while many such countries were increasing trade and investment connections with Cuba, the Bush administration was insisting that Cuba must be kept in international isolation. Most of Latin America defied Washington on this point, even going so far as to back Cuba's quest for a seat on the UN Security Council in 1989.

None of this made any difference to the shape of American foreign policy toward Cuba. Occasionally, there might be a shift in tactics, as when the administration decided to emphasize Cuba's human rights record or its lack of democracy rather than its alleged exportation of revolution. But the embargo stayed in place and was destined to be tightened, and further restrictions on travel and currency transactions were soon to be put in place. Radio and TV Martí (the latter inaugurated in the early 1990s) continued to be subsidized to the tune of tens of millions of dollars even though both were consistently jammed by Havana and a presidential task force had strongly recommended their termination. According to one Senate staffer: "Congress kept funding it because of the campaign contributions from the Cuban-American community."[10] The executive branch agreed with this logic.

The Role of Congress

Those most susceptible to lobby pressure are congressmen and senators. For them, as Tip O'Neill once said, all politics is local, and they are in a constant hunt for votes and campaign money. That is exactly what a well-organized and -funded interest group is best able to deliver. Thus, it was in Congress that one found the most extreme supporters of CANF and the most uncompromising demands for action against Cuba. With such demands, we can see the demise of any notion of national interest when weighed against the parochial interests of the powerful lobby.

During the administration of the senior George Bush, Congress—under the influence of such well-placed politicians as Florida's Bill McCollum, Connie Mack, and Bob Graham, Rhode Island's Claiborne Pell, New Jersey's Robert Torricelli, and North Carolina's Jesse Helms—sought to push the executive branch to enforce draconian measures that were arguably detrimental to the overall foreign policy and economic interests of the United States. For instance, while the administration's pressure on Gorbachev's Soviet Union—soon to be the Russia of Boris Yeltsin—had helped result in a steady shift away from the subsidization of Cuba, the pace was not fast enough for Congress. Thus, in the early 1990s, both Senate and House foreign operations appropriations bills involving aid to the Soviet Union were conditioned on that country's immediate suspension of all aid to Cuba.

To this position was added a reassertion of the Mack-Smith Amendments (found to be unworkable in the 1970s and already vetoed once by the president in 1990) that would ban overseas subsidiaries of American corporations from doing any business with Cuba. (This was a ban similar to the secondary aspects of the Arab boycott of Israel that the same U.S. politicians found so egregious.) There was no evidence that such a ban would seriously hurt the Castro regime, which could find alternative companies to supply its needs. It would, however, cost American subsidiaries an estimated $700 million a year in revenue. Perhaps more important, it put these subsidiaries in a position of not being able to carry on economic activities that were legal for other businesses in their host country. This could have a detrimental effect on the economy of the host country if the affected businesses represented large employers and investments. This, in turn, invited retaliation against the United States for restraint of trade in violation of international treaties. The European Commission (the executive arm of the European Union) described the Mack-Smith legislation as a "violation of the general principles of international law and the sovereignty of independent nations [with] the potential to cause grave damage to the transatlantic relationship."[11]

None of this mattered to Mas Canosa, who appeared before the House Foreign Relations Committee in 1992 demanding that the Congress close down subsidiary trade with Cuba. He also advocated that the United States pressure Mexico and Canada to cease trade with Cuba. Soon thereafter, Robert Torricelli introduced legislation, based on a draft proposal drawn up by Mas Canosa, to tighten the embargo.[12] Identical legislation was introduced in the Senate. This legislation was entitled the Cuban Democracy Act (CDA). Among other things, it forbade subsidiary trading. To the extent that the president sought to prevent potential damage to the Western trading alliance rather than make what Torricelli termed "the tough choices" on Cuba, he would be seen as a failed leader by CANF.[13]

It is to be noted that there was simply inadequate domestic opposition to this draconian bill. As Morley and McGillion tell us, some opposition came from grain-producing states as well as from those states with companies whose subsidiaries were endangered. The latter, however, were reluctant to go public with their arguments because of fear that they would be picketed and publicly castigated by Cuban American militants. Protest was made by small, moderate Cuban American organizations such as the Cuban American Committee, but this was done against the backdrop of public indifference underscored by continuing media news stylizations of Castro and his regime as outmoded and yet a continuing threat. Under these circumstances, all CANF's opposition was "comprehensively defeated."[14]

The Role of Political Opportunism

President Bush Sr. gave in to the demands of CANF as much as he could. However, unlike congressmen and senators, he was forced to consider a bigger picture when the country's major trading partners, functioning as a de facto counterlobby to CANF, drew a line in the sand and warned of retaliation if the United States tried to extend its law to cover the practices of economic entities operating on their soil. The president would back the CDA only if it were modified to give the White House some discretion over the implementation of its more draconian provisions—and, thus, avoid a confrontation with allied trading partners. Here, it might be argued, Bush may have had something like the national interest at heart. Alas, in Congress's collective heart, there was no compartment labeled *national interest*. Whatever the reason for Bush's behavior, it alienated CANF and its congressional allies and opened space for the president's political rivals. At this time, 1992, that chiefly meant Bill Clinton.

In April 1992, Clinton told a gathering of potential Cuban American contributors that the Bush administration had "missed a big opportunity to put the hammer down on Fidel Castro and Cuba" and that, if he became president, he would, unlike Bush, unequivocally support the CDA.[15] Soon, the Cuban American communities in Florida and New Jersey were contributing heavily to the Clinton presidential campaign. Come the election, many Cuban Americans would vote Democratic.

After his election in 1992, Clinton felt that he had won the presidency with the help of the Cuban American community. This translated into a sense of political obligation and dependence that made it impossible to respond favorably both when Castro sent signals (including the easing of travel restrictions on human rights activists) that it was ready to talk to the Democratic president and when moderates among the Cuban American community also approached the White House asking for a relaxation of the embargo and negotiations with Havana. Clinton was unable to respond to these overtures because the criterion determining policy on Cuba was not the national interest. That is, the national interest was not a consideration sufficient to reach a reasonable resolution of differences between the United States and Cuba. The criterion for action was maintenance of the goodwill of a powerful domestic lobby that could assist the Democrats in maintaining political power. As Clinton's new assistant secretary of state for inter-American affairs, Alexander Watson, remarked: "For the United States Cuba is not a foreign policy issue. Most of the time it's a domestic policy issue."[16]

Being a domestic issue meant that the political weakness of the moderate Cuban Americans made them as impotent as Castro when it came to effecting change in U.S. government policy. According to a National Security Council official of this period: "The moderate Cuban Americans were . . . disorganized and [prone to use] too much left-wing rhetoric." The hard-liners, on the other hand, were quite well organized, as an October 1993 demonstration of 100,000 anti-Castro Cubans in Miami made plain. This balance made it clear to people in the State Department and elsewhere in the government that compromise with Castro was, as Richard Nuccio, an adviser to Watson, put it, "a losing issue": "There [is] not some great constituency out there that is going to applaud you and, more importantly, promote your confirmation for higher office because you did the right thing on Cuba."[17]

As a consequence of this situation, Secretary of State Warren Christopher told a press conference early on in his tenure that there would be no compromise with Castro because he was "a relic of the past . . . mired in communist ideologies of an earlier day."[18] The possibility that it was American policy that was "a relic of the past" was a politically impossible thought given the power of the Cuba lobby. As President Clinton sought to remind the Cuban Americans: "No Democrat in my lifetime, in the White House at least, has come close to taking the strong position I have [on] Cuba."[19] Vice President Al Gore made it clear that the administration's policy would be to convince the people of Cuba to conclude that their present government was "an abject failure."[20] Deputy Assistant Secretary of State Michael Skol told Congress: "The point of the embargo was to impoverish the government [of Cuba] . . . to make sure that when Castro's end comes there would be insufficient movement to make possible a continuation of the regime." According to Morley and McGillion, the impoverishing of the regime in Cuba meant that the Cubans themselves would have to suffer under "the same blunt instrument that had been wielded by previous administrations: economic warfare."[21]

The Clinton Administration Confronts Old Issues

Sparking a Refugee Crisis

Unfortunately, for the Clinton administration, there were ways in which the Castro government could retaliate for this program of impoverishment. The American policy, even more than the policies of the regime, made life in Cuba hard for many, particularly those who were desirous of a middle-class standard of living. Thus, there were always people seeking to leave the island. On the other hand, the number of visas issued by the U.S. interests section in Havana never met the demand, and the process could be periodically slowed down to cause trouble for the Cuban authorities. The result was, sometimes, a rash of attempted hijackings of ships and planes. In August 1994, a Cuban naval officer was killed during just such a hijacking, and the Cuban authorities asked for the murderer's extradition. Washington refused. In response, the Cuban government halted all efforts to prevent their citizens from taking to the sea in rafts, small boats, and the like. Within two days, a refugee crisis reminiscent of the Mariel exodus of 1980 was in progress. The waters between Cuba and Florida were filled with hundreds of rafts and thousands of refugees.[22]

Though the Clinton administration tried to blame Castro for the refugee crisis, the political problem was all Washington's. There was a real possibility of a non–Cuban voter backlash (a potential counterconstituency to CANF) at the prospect of thousands of unexpected Cuban immigrants flooding Florida. This was something both the Clinton administration and the governor of Florida, Lawton Chiles, wanted to avoid. As a consequence, the rafters were taken to Guantanamo naval base as a safe haven. In an interview with President Clinton on August 19, Mas Canosa suggested that the proper response to the situation was a "full blockade" of Cuba.[23] The president did not want to go this far but promised to tighten the embargo even further. As Morley and McGillion point out, it was the embargo policy that "arguably bore the greatest responsibility for the crisis itself."[24]

As the crisis grew worse for the American government, the Cuban government offered to open talks with the United States on all contested issues, including the embargo. Pleas now came from Cuban Catholic bishops, human rights and dissident organizations, and even some of the more reasonable elements in Congress for the government to negotiate. Clinton flatly refused to take up this diplomatic invitation and dispatched several emissaries to Miami to assure CANF officials that no broad talks would be held with Castro. However, Washington was forced to eventually enter into eight days of talks with Havana specific to the crisis. In exchange for Cuba's halting the exodus, Washington was obliged to cease its manipulation of the visa process and immediately accept twenty thousand Cuban refugees. By late September, the rafters had disappeared from the waters off Florida.

The Helms-Burton Act

As the refugee crisis of 1994 indicated, maintaining the status quo on Cuba meant that the Clinton administration would inevitably meet with some of the same dilemmas that had confronted its predecessors. And among them were problems of trade policy that precluded giving the Cuba lobby and its congressional allies all that they desired. The most dramatic problem was the issue of subsidiary and foreign trade with Cuba and the loophole in the embargo that it constituted. This was due to the influence of, combined with not so subtle threats by, European and American continent trading partners who together constituted a de facto counterlobby to CANF. It will be recalled that this was the situation that alienated Mas Canosa and his congressional allies from the senior President Bush.

Initially, the Clinton administration took a hard line with its trading partners on the issue of subsidiary trade. Cables were sent to all U.S. embassies instructing them to warn their respective host governments that increased trade with Cuba would draw a negative reaction from the

United States. Dennis Hays, Clinton's director of the Office of Cuban Affairs, has been described as an advocate of the "kick them in the nuts to gain their attention school of diplomacy." This being the case, he "wanted to go around and tell the governments [of the world] don't you know who we are, don't you know who you are messing with?"[25]

However, the European Union, Canada, and the countries of Central and South America refused to be intimidated. As far as they were concerned, Cuba was no longer a threat to anyone, a position with which, much to the embarrassment of the administration, the Pentagon agreed. Therefore, in the European Union report on trade barriers, released in April 1993, the CANF-sponsored CDA was pointedly cited as an example of American politicians' willingness to essentially negate their own country's trade laws for the sake of "domestic concerns." The European position was that Cuba was making incremental steps toward political and economic reform and that the best way to encourage this was through positive engagement. The UN special rapporteur for Cuba, Carl-Johan Groth, agreed with this position. In his 1993 annual report, he wrote: "A policy . . . based on economic sanctions . . . designed to isolate the island constitute[s] . . . the surest way of prolonging an untenable internal situation." This was because it would leave the Cuban regime with but one acceptable option, and that was to "stay anchored in the past."[26]

CANF and its congressional allies were deaf to these arguments. And, after the midterm elections of 1994, those allies were stronger than ever as the Republicans came to control both houses of Congress. Early in 1995, Senator Jesse Helms of North Carolina, who was now chairman of the Senate Foreign Relations Committee, and Indiana's Dan Burton, who now ran the House Western Hemisphere Subcommittee, teamed up to produce the Cuban Liberty and Democratic Solidarity Act (otherwise known as the Helms-Burton Act). The legislation sought to increase Cuba's international economic isolation and to get compensation for the American owners of property expropriated during the revolution (whether they still wanted it or not). Thus, under the bill, foreign firms that made use of such property were open to suit in U.S. courts, they could lose their ability to do business in the United States, and their executives (whom Helms and Burton liked to describe as those who "trafficked" in stolen property) could be denied entrance into the country. The bill also took a swipe at

Russia by legislating that the U.S. government was to withhold from any assistance plan the equivalent of aid rendered to Havana by Russia in return for the use of the intelligence-gathering facility at Lourdes, Cuba. The Pentagon pointed out that the Russians used that facility to verify arms control agreements and that to deny them the ability to do so would not be in the national interest. On this issue, Helms and Burton made the requirement subject to presidential waiver.

Two facts are to be noted at this point. First, Fidel Castro had, repeatedly, sought to resolve disputed U.S. property claims through negotiation (as he had successfully done in the case of Canada and various European countries). But Washington, tied to the Cuba lobby's insistence that there be no bilateral talks with Havana, had always refused to negotiate. Second, according to Assistant Secretary of State Alexander Watson, most of the U.S. corporations that had held expropriated properties in prerevolutionary Cuba were no longer interested in pursuing claims against the Cuban government.[27] These facts also meant little to Helms, Burton, and CANF.

What the Helms-Burton Act primarily aimed at was to make it difficult for anyone doing business in the United States, including the foreign subsidiaries of U.S.-based corporations, to do business with Cuba. And they wanted President Clinton's cooperation in this effort. This demand would, of course, confront Clinton with the same dilemma that had faced Bush.

Initially, at least, Clinton chose not to confront the Cuba lobby and its allies. This willingness to give in to the lobby was enhanced by the fact that, in January 1966, two planes belonging to the Cuban exile group Brothers to the Rescue had, in defiance of earlier warnings, illegally flown into Cuban airspace and dropped leaflets over Havana calling for anti-government demonstrations. The Cubans proceeded to shoot the planes down. The uproar in Congress over the shoot-down (not the illegal behavior of the Cuban exiles) made opposition to Helms-Burton politically impossible. Thus, Clinton would sign the bill, and an effort would be made to convince trading partners to accept the American point of view or, at least, as Morley and McGillion put it, "attach some conditionality to any cooperation accord they signed with Havana." Once signed, the American embargo ceased to be policy and became law. As Morley and McGillion remark, the embargo could now be lifted only if "a democratic government (as defined by the bill) came to power in Cuba or when the Congress, of its own accord, agreed to pass another act rendering Helms-Burton null and void."[28]

Facing the Trade Dilemma

The Helms-Burton Act allowed the president to waive the implementation of Title III of the bill (the part calling for action against those "trafficking" in expropriated Cuban property) for six-month periods. In August 1996, able to delay no longer, Clinton issued his first such waiver. In doing so, he knew that he was risking his political position in Florida and New Jersey in the upcoming presidential election, but he also knew that to (as Congressman Lincoln Diaz-Balart put it) "show some backbone" and not use the waiver would risk a trade war with America's closest allies.[29]

In early June 1996, the Canadian prime minister, Jean Chrétien, made it clear both to his countrymen and to the U.S. government that he would not stand by idly and allow Washington to dictate Canada's trade practices. This, he said, was literally the "extraterritorial application of American law."[30] In South America, the fourteen-nation Rio Group declared that Helms-Burton "violates principles and norms established by international laws and the UN and the Organization of American States Charters [while it] ignores the basic principle of respect for the sovereignty of other states."[31] As for the European Union, whose trade with the United States certainly constituted an American national interest, it collectively rejected Helms-Burton in what one U.S. official called "the most undiplomatic language I've ever seen."[32] The EU officials made it known to President Clinton that, if Helms-Burton was activated and used against their countries' businesses, there would certainly be tough retaliatory actions taken.

Thus, it was the conviction, brought home to him by the de facto counterlobby of trading partners, that Helms-Burton posed too great a risk to the U.S. economy and long-standing trading alliances that prompted Clinton to use the Title III waiver. It was a brave act considering that his reelection campaign was ongoing and Florida was a key state in the race. In this regard, the president got an assist from the weather when, in mid-October 1996, Hurricane Lili hit Cuba and he could show himself concerned with the fate of the Cuban people by making a series of humanitarian gestures. Thus, in the end, he actually won Florida by 6 percentage points.

Holding to Custom and Tradition

Having won reelection despite his use of the Title III waiver, Clinton was now in a good position to defy the congressional anti-Castro radicals and initiate new, and saner, policies toward Cuba. He would have been helped along by the fact that Mas Canosa had died in November 1997 at the age of fifty-eight, leaving CANF in the hands of his less authoritative son. And, as we will shortly see, he would have found willing allies in the U.S. corporate world. Nonetheless, it soon became clear that, unless confronted with the most dire consequences (such as a trade war with allies), he was as tied to the customary and traditional approach to Cuba as were his congressional colleagues. He had no stomach for confronting the anti-Castro cabal in Congress and, therefore, maintained old policies that were designed to appease it.

This failure to move in a new direction seemed inexplicable to an increasingly frustrated American business community, which viewed Cuba as a small but potentially lucrative market the potential profits from which were being squandered for the sake of political expediency. Willard Workman, the vice president of the U.S. Chamber of Commerce, observed: "By and large, most American companies look at the Cuba embargo and say basically it doesn't make sense, it hasn't worked, it is inconsistent with our approach to other communist countries and the stated foreign policy objective, which is to have a change in political regime—clearly, it's been a dismal failure."[33] Indeed, noting that some thirty-five countries had come under some form of economic sanctions by the U.S. government in just three years (1993–1996), the business community was starting to wonder whether expanding profits for American companies was still seen as a national interest. Clearly, unless it began to act as a strong and united lobby group (which, in terms of Cuba, it had not), its interests were likely to become secondary to those of others.

In the meantime, the wishes of President Clinton, the U.S. business community, and the European Union were less than secondary to Senator

Helms, Representative Burton, and a slew of Cuban American legislators such as Lincoln Diaz-Balart and Ileana Ros-Lehtinen. They were busy conspiring on new legislation that would prevent Clinton from continuing to use the Title III waiver while demanding that the administration force the Europeans and others to play ball on Cuba. Though they were unable to achieve this goal, Clinton had to listen to repeated criticism for the remainder of his term from congressmen and senators who thought him weak willed relative to the Europeans and other trading partners. They also were in the habit of throwing tantrums whenever the Pentagon periodically declared that Cuba was no longer a threat to the United States or anyone else in the Western Hemisphere or the State Department failed to come up with any evidence that either Fidel Castro or his brother Raúl was involved in drug trafficking. As Morley and McGillion sadly observe: "The problem for the White House was that it was dealing with individuals for whom the numbers and evidence were not prerequisites for establishing the reality as they perceived it."[34]

In Comes George W. Bush

By the end of Clinton's second term, the Cuban American community had the same disappointed and disdainful opinion of his administration as it had once held of the senior George Bush. As a consequence, Vice President Al Gore's campaign for the presidency suffered. CANF and its followers turned their backs on Gore as tainted by Clinton's alleged weakness to go all the way to bring down Castro, and he lost Florida to George W. Bush in the 2000 elections.

The junior Bush entered the White House with the by-now familiar determination to "see the end of the Castro regime and the dismantling of the apparatus that has kept him in office for so long."[35] For the new president, the embargo against Havana was, as he put it, "not just a policy tool, [but] a moral statement."[36] He quickly made a series of appointments that placed right-wing ideologues like Otto Reich, Elliott Abrams, and John Negroponte, all of whom had been involved in supporting bloody and illegal covert wars in Central America, into positions that allowed them to influence Cuba policy. This was followed by support for legislation put forward by Jesse Helms and Joseph Lieberman that would funnel $100 million to anti-Castro groups. This effort constituted, according to one congressional staff member, "a covert aid program" the purpose of which was to promote internal subversion in Cuba.[37]

George W. Bush also created a Commission for Assistance to a Free Cuba. In May 2004, the commission brought in its recommendations embedded within a five-hundred-page report. It assumed, as had the last two administrations, that the Castro regime was close to collapse and that all that was needed to bring it down was to ratchet up the pressure. Two years later, President Castro was still in place, and the plan was being reworked by Secretary of State Condoleezza Rice. Its goal was now to assist disaffected Cubans to overthrow the regime from within. Rice supplied a long list of recommended actions and promised U.S. support if the Cuban people cared to put her theory of rebellion into practice. She also suggested that the Cuban dissidents time their efforts to match the assumed approaching demise of the old and ailing Fidel—efforts that would somehow prevent his brother Raúl from succeeding him. CANF and right-wing Miami Cuban leaders confidently assumed that the Castro government would fall when its founder died.

Like all previous predictions of the fall of the Castro regime, this one too turned out to be wrong. At the end of July 2006, too ill to govern any longer, Fidel turned over control of the government to Raúl. There were no uprisings, no protests, no internal calls for U.S. intervention. The succession went smoothly, and Cuba went on as before. So did the American government, which was no more willing to negotiate with Raúl Castro than with Fidel. Instead, the Bush administration continued the policies of its predecessors: the expansion of Radio and TV Martí (both of which have a twenty-year record of ineffectiveness), an $80 million fund for those opposing the Havana regime (the vast majority of which remains in the coffers of Miami-based dissidents), and greater travel restrictions (which made family visits legal only once every three years).

More indicative of the Bush administration posture toward both Cuba and the CANF/Cuban American elites is the ongoing case of Luis Posada Carriles. Carriles, who was in the hands of U.S. customs officials but released on bail in April 2007, is a terrorist operative and ex-CIA agent who was involved in the bombing of a Cuban civilian airliner in 1976. That attack killed seventy-three innocent people, including a number of Venezuelans. In 2005, Venezuela asked for his extradition on a charge of terrorism. The United States has an extradition treaty with Venezuela and, thus, is legally obligated to comply unless the Bush administration itself wishes to put him on trial. The White House has chosen to do neither, temporizing while it hunts for a friendly third-party country willing to take him. To send Carriles to Venezuela, a country with which the Bush administration has an ongoing war of words, or to try him for terrorism here in the United States would run against the administration's neoconservative ideology as well as cause a political breach with the equally right-wing Cuban American elite. In other words, despite the fact that George W. Bush has declared that those who harbor terrorists are themselves terrorists, it would seem that his administration has found it politically expedient to harbor a terrorist.

Even as all this hard-line behavior went forward, the same weakness (from the point of view of hard-line anti-Castro legislators) appeared in the junior Bush's Cuba policy as had shown up in the policies of his father and President Clinton. "Title III is the meat" of the embargo effort, one congressional staffer declared.[38] Secretary of State Colin Powell had told the House International Relations Committee that waivers of the Title III clause of the Helms-Burton Act would be given "only when we believe there are serious, great, overriding national interests for which waiver authority is provided."[39] Nonetheless, on July 16, 2001, this otherwise fire-breathing administration announced the first of a series of six-month waivers of Title III. The administration had met with the same formidable counterlobby pressure as had its predecessors. Such pressure is the only thing that Washington politics, at least at the executive branch level, seems to respond to. Otherwise, what has become the custom and tradition of Washington's Cuba foreign policy goes on and on.

In the meantime, the Cuban economy had passed through its transition phase following the halt in Soviet/Russian aid. It was now growing at roughly 8 percent per year, and tourism was a strong growth industry. The country had found markets for its goods (including nickel, which had replaced sugar as the main raw material export) and established a strong barter-based trading relationship with Venezuela. In other areas, Havana signed twelve UN-sponsored treaties designed to fight international terrorism. The Russians had closed down their electronic listening post at Lourdes and evacuated their remaining fifteen hundred troops. These moves did not translate into reciprocal action in Washington, such as the removal of Cuba from the State Department's list of states supporting terrorism or an end to the repeated claim that Cuba was a security threat. After all, as many had noted, Cuba was a domestic policy issue, and the domestic balance of power in reference to it had not changed.

Conclusion

America's Cuba policy has been, as Willard Workman noted, "a dismal failure." As a consequence, Colonel Lawrence Wilkerson, Colin Powell's former chief of staff, has called it "the dumbest policy on the face of the earth."[40] However, it is only a failure and dumb if judged by the criteria of its publicly stated goals as a foreign policy—that is, to isolate the Castro regime and, by doing so, cause its collapse. If looked on in another way, as a domestic policy, it can be judged a success. In other words, if the goal of both Republican and Democratic politicians is to cater to a powerful domestic lobby so as to procure its electoral and financial support, then (in an alternating sort of way: one political season the support goes to the Democrats, the next to the Republicans) this end has been achieved. It is to be noted that, in the successful pursuit of this domestic political goal, almost all other national interest–related foreign policy goals have been rendered irrelevant. The profit-making capitalist ambitions of the agricultural sector, among others, of the U.S. economy have been ignored, the pleas of moderates that American policy has made the work of in-country Cuban dissidents much harder have been ignored, the aid that Cuba was willing to render in both the War on Drugs and the War on Terror has been ignored, and the benefits of maximizing transitional aid to Russia have been ignored.

If these aspects of what might be deemed national interest had no ability to change the U.S. government's political behavior in the case of Cuba policy, the actions of a strong counterlobby did. The stand taken by key allies—that they would not tolerate the extraterritorial application of U.S. law to their own economies—was the only remedy to the power of the Cuba lobby. In other words, the only thing that can counter lobby power in Washington was and is equal or greater counterlobby power.

It is significant that, in this case, the counterlobby came from outside the United States. In other words, one of the characteristics of an enduring and consistently successful special interest is its ability to hold competitive domestic interest groups at bay. Often, this is done through intimidation and threat, with the result that, in the case at hand, even a broad array of economic interests refused to risk the picketing and name-calling that came along with a direct challenge to hard-line Cuban activists. Thus, America's Cuba policy remains privatized, and little of any note has actually been accomplished in relation to that island nation. To date, the United States is simply stuck in a faction-induced rut when it comes to Cuba.

By 2007, this rut had generated increased opposition within the Cuban American community itself. This opposition seems to reflect a generational split between those who came to the United States in the original wave of immigrants following Castro's seizure of power (these are the hard-liners who proudly fashion themselves part of *el exilio histórico*) and younger, second- and third-generation Cuban Americans born in the United States. Polls indicate that a majority of the latter group would like to see an easing of boycott restrictions against Cuba, particularly travel restrictions, and an encouragement of gradual, rather than abrupt and violent, change in Cuba.[41] However, it is one of the premises of this book that the opinions of the majority do not necessarily make, or lead to a change in, government policy. The influential Cuban American lobbies (CANF has now been displaced by the U.S. Cuba Democracy Political Action Committee, led by Mauricio Claver-Carone) still insist on a mostly hard-line agenda. Their influence is reflected in a speech given by George W. Bush at the State Department on October 25, 2007. Insisting that the present Cuban government is a "disgraced and dying order," the president refused to compromise on the sanctions now in place: "America will have no part in giving oxygen to a criminal regime victimizing its own people." He dismissed the recent transfer of power from Fidel to Raúl Castro as "the old way with new faces" and directly appealed to the Cuban people to "rise up to demand liberty."[42]

This particular example of a privatized and dumb policy has mostly affected Cuba's economic development and, thus, the standard of living of its people. It may also have prevented any political evolution away from one-party rule because of a predictable tendency to clamp down on dissent in the face of a constant external threat. While U.S. foreign policy toward Cuba has had its violent side (after all, the U.S. government did sponsor the Bay of Pigs invasion and several attempts to assassinate Fidel Castro), it has not resulted in ravaged populations and open warfare.

Unfortunately, in other parts of the world, particularly the Middle East, running a foreign policy that reflects the parochial interests of a powerful lobby has had much more serious consequences. These do include death, destruction, war, and, generally, ongoing disaster for an entire region of the globe.

5

Privatizing National
Interest—the Israel Lobby

The ancestors of a majority of American Jews come from Europe. The
European Jews are known as the Ashkenazim and, of all the world's Jews,
they were the ones who suffered the most consistent and harshest anti-
Semitism and persecution. Their history has included a long period of
persecution in czarist Russia, pogroms in much of Eastern Europe, and
the Dreyfus Affair in France and culminated in the Nazi Holocaust. This
history has largely conditioned the outlook of American Jews and instilled
in them a collective feeling of vulnerability that is more or less conscious
depending on the conditions of the time.

Small numbers of European Jews came to the British colonies of
North America as early as the eighteenth century. And, like the other elements of the colonial population that had come looking for religious freedom, they brought their memories of persecution with them. However,
unlike those of the Protestant colonists who went on to make up most
of the nation's ruling elite, the memories of the Jewish colonists never
completely faded, even in a political environment, described by George
Washington in a 1790 letter to the local synagogue of Newport, Rhode
Island, as one in which the government "gives to bigotry no sanction, to
persecution no assistance."[1]

Washington was speaking of the federal government of which he was
the first president. Yet, until the mid-twentieth century, such power as
would immediately affect the lives of citizens resided at the state and lo-

cal levels. And, as the history of slavery, Jim Crow laws, Red Scares, the women's suffrage movement, and the civil rights struggle of the 1960s tells us, there was plenty of active bigotry, paranoia, and persecution at these levels.[2] Just enough of this affected the Jews to maintain a low-level feeling of insecurity. In the fight against the discriminatory tendencies of the majority, the Jewish elites (which, in the nineteenth century and the early twentieth, were of German origin)[3] would use the courts and occasionally ally with others (at first Catholics and later African Americans) to beat back debilitating laws and practices. These efforts naturally gave rise to "defensive" organizations.

One of the earliest of these organizations was the Board of Delegates of American Israelites (founded in 1859), which established the tactical pattern of government lobbying. The board was relatively successful. For instance, it was due to its lobbying effort that an 1860s proposal for a constitutional amendment declaring the United States "a Christian nation" failed to pass Congress. The activities of the board marked the emergence of a generation of American Jews who no longer saw themselves as newcomers on the American political scene, instead feeling established enough to operate as insiders.[4] Their lobbying and other political activities were aimed at making the United States as tolerant and open a society for all citizens as possible. They knew that it was in their community interest to make domestic tolerance a national interest.

In 1878, the Board of Delegates merged with the Union of American Hebrew Congregations (UAHC). This merger attests to the continuing dominance of Jews whose religious values and customs of worship were traditionally oriented. However, by the late nineteenth century, Reform Judaism, a less traditionalist and increasingly Americanized form of Judaism, emerged. For instance, the Reform Jews claimed to see the call for Jews to repossess Jerusalem as only a metaphor. They were Americans first and foremost. Deserted by the Reform Jews in 1883, the Board of Delegates/UAHC suffered yet another setback when the ultratraditionalists, the Orthodox Jews, left the organization later the same year.

Thus, by the 1880s, American Jewry was divided into three parts. Yet this schism reflected internal and somewhat esoteric disagreements and did not reflect any division about the vision for a tolerant and open American society. Thus, it did not prove a great challenge for Jewish Americans during this period. Nor, at this time, did any great challenge come from anti-Semitic American gentiles promoting discriminatory behavior. The greatest challenge would come from the mass exodus of Jews fleeing Russian and Eastern European persecution and the fact that the vast majority of these refugees (some two million) were heading for American shores. There is something sadly ironic, though politically logical, about the fact that the descendants of Jews who championed tolerance and whose ancestors had found refuge in colonial America a hundred years before now looked with anxiety on the arrival of this next wave of Jewish refugees.

The fear among the established Jewish community was that the arrival of so many alien Jews would stir up latent American anti-Semitism and erode the insider status of the established Jews. This reaction also had a certain class aspect. The Russian and East European Jews were poor and distinctive in their dress, manners, and speech. Some of them were also politically suspect, harboring socialist and anarchist sympathies. A small number were Zionists.[5]

To minimize the impact on their own higher class status and also help assimilate the newcomers as quickly as possible, the now three distinct Jewish communities produced yet more organizations, committees, and activist groups. Premier among them was the American Jewish Committee, which, while financing efforts to educate and employ the new arrivals, successfully lobbied the U.S. government to abrogate its bilateral trade treaty with Russia because of that nation's official discrimination against Jews. What is significant here is the way in which the American Jewish Committee presented its case. As J. J. Goldberg tells us: "The fight against the Russian trade treaty was presented as an American domestic issue. Russia's anti-Semitic laws extended not only to Russian Jews, but to American Jewish visitors as well."[6] This approach, essentially making a domestic case out of a foreign policy issue, would be a tactic used again and again by the Jewish lobby groups.

Another Jewish group established at this time (1913) was the Anti-Defamation League (ADL) of B'nai B'rith. As had been feared, the influx of Jewish immigrants had caused a rapid increase in the use of negative Jewish stereotypes in the newspapers of the day. B'nai B'rith set up the ADL to pressure the media not to use descriptions and images that denigrated Jews or identified them with disturbing developments (such as an increase in the crime rate). In the 1930s, the ADL transformed from a defensive organization to one with an "offensive" posture by establishing an intelligence-gathering arm that targeted anti-Semitic groups.

In the 1920s and 1930s, anti-Semitism was, indeed, on the rise in the United States, largely following a similar trend throughout the Western world. How closely this phenomenon matched the racial theories springing up in Europe can be seen in an article written by President Calvin Coolidge for *Good Housekeeping* magazine in the early 1920s in which he asserted: "Biological laws show us that Nordics deteriorate when mixed with other races."[7] Working from this pseudoscientific assumption, Coolidge signed the Johnson-Reed Immigration Reform Act of 1924, shutting down the immigration of non-Aryan groups, including Jews. It is this restrictive stand on immigration—supported by over 80 percent of the American people well into the 1940s—that prevented the United States from rescuing many Jews, and others as well, from Nazi persecution.

All the major American Jewish organizations of the day had, at least officially, opposed the harshly restrictive immigration law. Indeed, in 1924, the head of the American Jewish Committee, Louis Marshall, sought an appointment with Coolidge to urge him to veto the Johnson-Reed bill. Coolidge refused to see him. After this, Jewish opposition was restrained out of fear of an anti-Semitic backlash. There was, however, a Jewish group that refused to take any sort of stand against immigration restrictions. This was the American Zionists.

At this time (from 1920 to the mid-1930s), Zionist Jews were but a minority of the overall American Jewish community. As a group, they tended to stand apart from the other Jewish groups. They were largely silent on the immigration issue because, ideologically, they were opposed to Jews coming to the United States. They insisted, instead, that they should go to Palestine. Thus, closing the door to Palestine's most attractive competitor as a refuge for Jews was in their interest. They held to this position even as an awareness of Nazi genocide grew.[8]

World War II and the Holocaust enhanced a deepening sense of vulnerability in all of surviving Jewry. The episodes of "respectable" and sometimes intense anti-Semitic discrimination that had appeared in the United States during the interwar and World War II period added to American Jewish insecurities. Thus, American Jews felt that they were once more outsiders—even when, with the end of World War II, American feeling toward Jews reversed itself. J. J. Goldberg suggests: "Jews may have benefitted from widespread postwar revulsion against the evils of prejudice . . . coupled with a general mood of good-natured optimism that emerged from the victory over fascism and the booming economy of the 1950s."[9] Whatever the reasons, American Jewish organizations reacted to the recent past, and the new situation of the present, by adopting an aggressive posture toward anything that smacked of discriminatory behavior against minorities.

In the 1950s and 1960s, American Jewish organizations reallied with each other under new umbrella organizations such as National Jewish Community Relations Advisory Council, which encouraged the establishment of Jewish community relations committees throughout the United States. Jewish organizations also established alliances that fought for civil rights reforms in the 1960s. The previous thirty years had taught them that they could not rely on sweet reason alone to change the potentially dangerous prejudices that lurked within society. Those prejudices had to be attacked as well as defended against. As Goldberg puts it: "Quiet diplomacy was out; legal action was in."[10] American Jews responded enthusiastically to these campaigns, pouring millions of dollars into the coffers of the various organizations, as well as lending their time and energy to political work. This was the period when the Jews made their reputation as activists within postwar American politics.

It is to be noted that the evolution of the American Jewish civil and political posture, driven as it was by a sense of vulnerability, had its core references in the American domestic scene. The reaction to events abroad—whether the massive immigration at the turn into the twentieth century or, later, the refugee problem created by Nazi persecution—was determined by the Jewish experience in America. This is one reason why American Jews' relief efforts in the early years of the century were in good part motivated by their fear of the impact on their own status of continued Jewish immigration. It is also why, later on in the century, the behavior of the American Jewish organizations was sometimes inconsistent. Some, like the American Jewish Committee, were more conservative in their approach to domestic anti-Semitism and discrimination (always fearing that an aggressive reaction would only make things worse), while others, such as the American Jewish Congress, were more assertive. As things got worse in the 1930s and 1940s, the conservative posture prevailed, particularly on issues that referenced foreign situations. This is one reason why American Jews did not press harder for immigration reform even in the face of Nazi genocide. When the environment of American anti-Semitism abated, however, American Jewish organizations expressed a pent-up frustration with much more assertive action that, at least up until the year 1967, focused on domestic issues such as the fight for civil rights.

The American Zionists Emerge

This new assertiveness applying itself to the elimination of any pronounced discriminatory behavior within America's legal and social domestic environment was a productive posture. It led to purposeful alliances with other American minorities and certainly served the self-interest of the American Jewish community. Once more, the community understood that its interest was in fighting to make the vision of a tolerant America a national interest.

The one exception that had always existed to this position was the Zionist Organization of America (ZOA). It was, in essence, a one-issue organization. That issue was, not the interests of American Jewry, but promoting the Jewish colonization of Palestine and, after 1948, aiding Israel. Of course, all the major American Jewish organizations had supported Israel's creation and its continued existence. But, unlike the ZOA, they were not wholly fixated on what was, after all, a foreign policy issue. It was not until the 1960s that this began to change.

The Zionists had gained strength rapidly during World War II. For instance, ZOA membership in the year 1941 stood at about forty-six thousand, a figure that compared favorably with the other major Jewish organizations. This can be seen as a logical consequence of Jewish community frustration and fear. The frustration came from the inability, and often the unwillingness, of the mainstream Jewish groups to challenge the immigration laws that were stranding millions of Jews (often the relatives of American Jewish citizens) in an ever more hostile Europe. The fear came from the awareness that such restrictions reflected an ever more open American-style anti-Semitism. The logical conclusion to be drawn from all this appeared to be that the Zionists were right when they said that the Jews needed a state of their own. Thus, the war years brought greater support for the ZOA and, slowly but surely, saw most other Jewish organizations falling in line with Zionist programs.[11]

The American Zionists—whose aims did not reference the needs of domestic Jews—used this support to lobby both the American government and the American people themselves to support the transformation of Palestine into a Jewish homeland. When it came to selling this goal, the Zionists were spending some $70,000 a year in the 1940s to "crystallize the sympathy of Christian America" for the cause of a Jewish Palestine. They were also working hard to establish allied gentile organizations such as the American Palestine Committee, which, by 1941, boasted among its membership "68 senators, 200 congressmen and numerous academics, clergy and leaders in many walks of life."[12] As these numbers imply, the Zionists were particularly successful in the case of the U.S. Congress. Indeed, Palestine as a refuge for the Jews was very popular with American politicians in the 1930s and 1940s because it was a way of helping Jewish refugees, and, thus, assuaging the guilt that came along with draconian immigration statutes, without having to alter those statutes. Yet, as we will see, Palestine for the Jews was problematic in terms of what should have been American national interests even before the state of Israel was created.

The Problem of National Interests, Part 1

An early example of the complications that could arise from American political susceptibility to Zionist lobbying can be found in the case of the congressional resolutions of 1944. On January 27, 1944, at the behest of American Zionists, Representatives James A. Wright of Pennsylvania and Ranulf Compton of Connecticut introduced a resolution in the House of Representatives that urged the U.S. government to take "appropriate measures" to induce the British government to allow unlimited Jewish immigration into Palestine. According to Wright and Compton, this would result in the ultimate creation of "a free and democratic Jewish Commonwealth." A few days later, on February 1, an identical resolution was introduced into the Senate by Robert Wagner of New York and Robert Taft of Ohio. At the time, Wagner tied the resolution to what he saw as a history of congressional commitment to Zionism going back to Congress's 1922 joint resolution in support of the Balfour Declaration. Wagner went so far as to assert: "Although [the Balfour Declaration] was issued in the name of the British Government it was as a matter of fact a joint policy of the Governments of Great Britain and the United States." As a matter of fact, Wagner was wrong. America's association with the document went no further than a personal, and very casual, nod of approval on the part of Woodrow Wilson.[13]

At the Senate hearings on the 1944 congressional resolutions, Wagner brought in most of the heads of major Jewish organizations, the American Jewish Committee, the American Council for Judaism, and Rabbi Abba Silver for the Zionists. Interestingly enough, at this time, one could actually bring opponents of the Zionist position before Congress, so we find the historian Philip Hitti from Princeton University telling the senators, on February 15, that Zionist aims at transforming Palestine into a "Jewish Commonwealth" violated "the third article of the Atlantic Charter[, which recognizes] the right of people to choose their own government."[14]

Unfortunately for Hitti and the Palestinians, international law (then as now) carried little weight with Congress. The entire process of putting forth the resolutions and debating and passing them appeared preplanned and attested to the power of the Zionist movement by this time. One reason that the Zionists' lobby power worked so well was (and is) because all politics are local. Thus, Jewish lobbyists rallying local voters both Jewish and gentile, and using their financial wherewithal in shrewd political ways, could get their way on issues that had little or very weak organized opposition. Another reason was attested to by a *New York Times* editorial in support of the resolutions published on February 12, 1944, that stated: "The increasingly desperate state of those of the Jewish faith in Europe has made it more than ever evident that the . . . doors of any place of refuge . . . should be open wider." The *Times* conveniently overlooked the draconian restrictions on American immigration law and proceeded to castigate Great Britain for its "arbitrary ban" on immigration to Palestine.[15]

It was true that Great Britain had moved to restrict Jewish immigration into Palestine since just before the outbreak of World War II. This came in London's White Paper of 1939. The action was, indeed, a reversal from the position originally taken in the Balfour Declaration, one promising the establishment of a Jewish homeland in Palestine, but it was hardly "arbitrary" or a decision taken because of anti-Semitic prejudice. It was an act of recognition that, with a world war looming, the British Empire had to compete with the fascists for the allegiance of the entire Arab and Muslim world. It could not do so while allowing unlimited Jewish immigration into Palestine. As British military strategists had noted in January 1939: "We assume that . . . the necessary measures would be taken . . . in order to bring about a complete appeasement of Arab opinions in Palestine and in neighbouring countries. . . . If we fail to retain Arab goodwill at the outset of a war, no other measures which we can recommend will serve to influence the Arab States in favour of this country."[16]

The *Times* editors went on to assert: "The case for American intervention in this question is stronger than it was five years ago. The presence of our troops and supply depots in the Near East and our vital concern in peace and order in this strategic area give us a greater right to urge that the White Paper should now be abrogated."[17] It was a strange argument, for the presence of "our troops and supply depots" essentially put the United States in the same position as Great Britain relative to the need to maintain friendly wartime relations with Arabs and Muslims. This was obvious to the State Department's Division of Near Eastern Affairs and to the War Department, so they urged President Roosevelt and the executive branch of government not to interfere with British policy in Palestine.

In fact, noninterference was a matter of national interest as far as Secretary of War Henry Stimson was concerned. He had been informed by the State Department's Division of Near Eastern Affairs that passage of the resolutions was likely to "precipitate armed conflict in Palestine and other parts of the Arab world, endangering American troops," as well as "seriously prejudice, if not make impossible, important pending negotiations with Ibn Saud for the construction of a pipeline across Saudi Arabia, a development of utmost importance to the security of the United States." Thus, on February 7, 1944, Stimson wrote Tom Connally, the chairman of the Senate Foreign Relations Committee: "The subject of this resolution is a matter of deep military concern to the War Department. I feel that the passage of this resolution at the present time, or even any public hearings thereon, would be apt to provoke dangerous repercussions in areas where we have many vital military interests." Secretary of State Cordell Hull followed this up with a letter of his own to Connolly suggesting: "No further action on this resolution would be advisable at this time."[18]

This was no mere speculation on the part of Stimson and Hull. Arab governments had made it quite clear to American authorities that they considered pro-Zionist congressional resolutions provocative. As to the pending 1944 resolutions, protests had been lodged with the U.S. legations in Egypt, Iraq, Transjordan, Saudi Arabia, Lebanon, Syria, and Yemen. The Iraqi government had communicated directly with Senators Taft, Wagner, and Connally to the effect that "immigration of Jews into Palestine with the idea of turning it into a Jewish state would lead to disturbances there and would aid the efforts of enemy propagandists." This was essentially what General George Marshall, the army chief of staff, told the Senate Foreign Relations Committee in executive session on March 4, 1944.[19]

While Marshall's intervention was sufficient to force a temporary withdrawal of the resolutions, the sponsors remained under continuing pressure from the American Zionists. It would seem that the Zionists were more concerned with their own organizational and ideological interests than any war-related national interest. The politicians, in turn, saw national interest in terms of their own local electoral interests. Thus, the resolutions' sponsors, and particularly Senator Taft, reacted churlishly to their forced withdrawal. Taft lashed out at the Iraqis for having the audacity to share their concerns with Congress. He told the *New York Times*: "The Congress of the United States, which for more than a century has been able to reach its own conclusions without advice from officials of foreign nations, is fully able to reach a wise conclusion in this matter." It being the case that Marshall had told the Congress about the same thing as the Iraqis had, Taft could not restrain himself from questioning his judgment as well. By the end of March, therefore, the *New York Times* noted, Taft had taken issue "with the military critics of the proposal [Congress's pro-Zionist resolutions] who suggested that the action might weaken the position of Allied troops in North Africa and the Middle East." After confessing that he was "no expert on military affairs" and that he "[did] not know enough about the military conditions in North Africa to affirm or deny the alleged [*sic*] position of the Secretary of War and General Marshall," Taft proceeded to do just that, telling the *Times*: "I strongly suspect that the real objection [to the resolutions] is political and not military."[20]

It is a testimony to the strength of American Zionist lobbying by this time that it could reach to the White House when needed. Thus, within a week of the withdrawal of the resolutions, President Roosevelt was muddying the waters by authorizing the American Zionist leaders Stephen Wise and Abba Silver to release a statement in which he proclaimed: "The American government has never given its approval to the White Paper of 1939. . . . When future decisions are reached full justice will be done to those who seek a Jewish national home, for which our government and the American people have always had the deepest sympathy." This statement only renewed Arab concerns and sent the State Department scurrying for an explanation of the contradictory positions taken within the government. In the opinion of the head of the Division of Near East Affairs, Wallace Murray—as well as that of the Office of Strategic Services (the wartime predecessor of the CIA)—the behavior of the U.S. Congress when it came to pro-Zionist resolutions "led to a material weakening in the American psychological position in the Near East."[21] This was a judgment that seemed to reflect a real wartime national interest.

The American Zionists and the pro-Zionist congressional leaders either did not believe the judgment of the diplomatic and military experts or did not care. And this presents the possibility that they saw their own parochial interests as more important than the wartime national interest. The congressional leaders used Roosevelt's statement to resurrect the resolutions and, by the end of March, were arguing that the statement "overruled . . . the chief of Staff [General Marshall]." This position was reinforced when, in the summer of 1944, both the Republican and the Democratic party platform committees inserted planks favoring the "opening of Palestine to unrestricted immigration and colonization."[22] As a consequence, the pro-Zionist resolutions were back on the floor of Congress by November.

By that time, the Arab diplomatic protests over the issue had transformed themselves into charges of betrayal by the U.S. government. These charges referred specifically to Roosevelt's promise that no decision would be taken altering the status of Palestine without prior consultation with both Arabs and Jews.[23] Such reminders forced Roosevelt to once more intervene to have the resolutions temporarily shelved.

The saga of the 1944 resolutions points to the fact that, even in the midst of a global war, Congress lived in an altogether different world than either the State or the War departments. These organizations dealt with international realities and the contending forces of an ongoing conflict. They could see the potential damage the resolutions were likely to have on the Allies' strategic military position, and, later, on the long-term overall interests of the United States, in the Middle East. On the other hand, it is hard to escape the conclusion that neither the American Zionists nor their supporters in Congress paid any attention to these issues unless absolutely forced to by General Marshall and, belatedly, President Roosevelt. And, even then, they did so begrudgingly and were constantly on the lookout for ways to get out from under limits imposed by strategic considerations.

Here, then, we have an example of the fact that the forces that shape behavior in the U.S. Congress are basically parochial in nature. The demands of the Zionist lobby may have presented a danger to U.S. national interests abroad, but they had become vital aspects of the interests of congressmen and senators at home. Therefore, they, and not U.S. national interests as defined by the foreign policy and military arms of the government, defined the behavior of most local politicians.[24] From this time on, this response pattern to Zionist lobbying would become fixed. For the Congress, and the political parties as well, Palestine/Israel would become an obsession.

The Postwar Situation

As we have seen, after the war, the Jewish organizations took a very aggressive position when it came to discriminatory domestic laws. They made alliances and helped promote civil rights for all citizens. However, as could be anticipated from the now permanent position of strength that the Zionist element occupied within the Jewish community, the maintenance of an uncritical, supportive attitude on the part of both the American people and the U.S. government toward the state of Israel was at least as important. This dual position can be seen as a two-pronged expression of continuing feelings of vulnerability. One had to fight for one's position in America as well as for the strong Israeli state, which could serve as a refuge if the future turned bad in America, as it once had in Germany. This was the psychological situation as the year 1967 approached. The events of that year would create a contradiction between these dual ends of the Jewish organizations. In that year, they would have to choose between continuing to work toward a liberal and tolerant America and uncritical support for Israel.

By the beginning of June 1967, Egypt and Israel were on the brink of war. Egyptian President Nasser's precipitous action in dismissing the UN peacekeeping forces in the Sinai Desert and closing the Strait of Tiran to Israeli shipping had contributed to this situation, as had Israel's hostile behavior toward Egypt's ally Syria. Under these circumstances, the Israelis initiated war with a predawn attack on Egypt in early June. Within six days, they had defeated the armies of Egypt, Syria, and Jordan and occupied the West Bank, Gaza, and the Golan Heights.

This victory was a surprise to everyone except the military and political experts who paid attention to the realities of the Middle East. The worldwide Jewish consensus flowed not from present reality (which the experts knew was characterized by Israeli strength and Arab weakness) but from historically conditioned feelings of vulnerability that encompassed not only the Israeli public but the diaspora too. As far as world Jewry was concerned, Israel was perpetually on the brink of annihilation—an assumption often encouraged by the American media. In the three weeks of crisis preceding the war, this fear of the imminent destruction of Israel reached fever pitch. However, instead of experiencing another Holocaust, what the Jews got was the rapid and complete victory of the Zionist state. This outcome produced both disorientation and delirious joy. And, in its mythic power, it confirmed and deepened the bond between almost all diaspora Jews and the Jewish state. A suggestion of this could be seen in the outpouring of American Jewish wealth that went to the United Jewish Appeal to help defray Israeli war expenses—$307 million in the six months following the war.[25]

As J. J. Goldberg points out, the rapid, if unexpected, victory of Israel did not leave American Jews with a greater sense of security. Rather: "The events of May and June 1967 shattered the nerves of the American Jewish community." Goldberg quotes the Jewish leader Milton Himmelfarb writing in *Commentary* in October 1967 to the effect that Jews had a "sudden realization that genocide, antisemitism, a desire to murder Jews—all those things were not merely what one had been taught about the bad, stupid past. . . . Those things were real and present." Jews had, Himmelfarb concluded, "relearned the old truth that you can depend only on yourself."[26]

It was this emotionally driven worldview (the Jews' ethnocentric thought collective) that dictated the response of American Jewish leaders to what happened next. The Israeli victory was not all positive. It gave Israel control of conquered territory that it almost immediately started to colonize, in violation of international law. More than a million non-Jews, that is, native Palestinians, found themselves under an increasingly oppressive regime of occupation. Israel was taken to task on human rights issues by the United Nations, and many Third World nations started to criticize Israeli policies in the newly occupied territories as resembling the behavior of apartheid South Africa.

Some of this criticism came from civil rights and antiwar groups in the United States with whom the American Jewish organizations had long-standing alliances. This proved to be the pivotal moment. Would the American Jewish leaders and activists stay true to their liberal principles of tolerance and equality for all, including the Palestinians under Israeli occupation, or would they retreat into a fortress mentality that interpreted all criticism of Israel as anti-Semitism and proof that the Jews could depend only on themselves? The answer turned out to be the latter. With little debate or hesitation, the establishment leadership of American Jewry traded its traditional alliances with the progressive forces of the nation for new alliances with right-wing conservative forces that uncritically backed Israel.

This was, perhaps, not an unexpected choice. If American Jewish leaders assumed that a strong Israel was forever on the brink of destruction, if they did not have the collective ego strength to accept others' criticism of postwar Israeli policies, and if they had no faith in the historically demonstrated ability of liberal policies to guarantee their own domestic rights, then a fortress mentality was the only thing they could retreat to. And so they did. Jewish leaders resigned from the liberal organizations that raised even the mildest criticism of Israel. And those few American Jews who kept to their liberal principles were accused of being traitors to their people.

Simultaneously, a new "holocaust awareness" sprung up among American Jews fueled by Israel's alleged recent "near death experience."[27] Jewish leaders started demanding that Holocaust studies become part of secondary and college curricula. Synagogues and Hebrew schools gave the topic a much greater place in their teachings and sermons. The Holocaust, which had been a symbol of a past overcome by a better present, was now put forth as a symbol of present and future danger. The Arabs were transformed into latter-day Nazis.

It is unclear what percentage of the general American Jewish population immediately went along with this rapidly developing dogma. However, there is little doubt that the vast majority of American Jews at least passively acquiesced in the policy shift. The shift was based on simple subtraction. Where before the 1967 war there were two pillars of American Jewish policy—Israel and the fight for a liberal and tolerant America—now there was only one. And that was Israel.

Zionism Triumphant

From this time on, the major goal of American Jewish organizations and lobbies was to serve the interests of Israel. All lobbies were now essentially Zionist. As far as Israeli leaders were concerned, this was only as it should be. From their point of view, the gentile world was inherently, if sometimes latently, hostile, and, therefore, Jewish organizations in the diaspora had no other purpose but to support the state of Israel. That is, all Jewish organizations in the diaspora should function in their home countries as agents of a foreign power. In the United States, the organization that now came to the fore in this role was the American Israel Public Affairs Committee (AIPAC). As a testimony to this claim, the AIPAC Web site quotes the *New York Times* describing it as "the most important organization affecting America's relationship with Israel."[28]

AIPAC was originally founded as the Washington-based office of the ZOA. At that time, the DC office was called the American Zionist Committee for Public Affairs. Its name was changed to the American Israel Public Affairs Committee in 1959. The initial head of the American Zionist Committee/AIPAC was Isaiah Kenen, an American journalist. Kenen had several times previously registered with the U.S. Justice Department as an agent of the American section of the Jewish Agency, a quasi-government organization based in Israel.[29] He had also worked as the press secretary and public relations person for the Israeli ambassador to the United Nations. This was the famed Abba Eban. It was Eban who first approached Kenen about setting up a lobbying effort to influence the U.S. government in Israel's favor. Together with Louis Lipsky, the leader of the American Zionist Council, the American Zionist Committee for Public Affairs was established with Kenen at its head. According to Lipsky, Kenen was to be an "American lobbyist for an American organization" and, thus, avoid the "impropriety of an agent of a foreign power lobbying Congress." However, according to revelations made during William Fulbright's Senate Foreign Relations Committee hearings in 1963, the Jewish Agency provided the start-up money and continued to subsidize the American Zionist Committee/AIPAC indirectly through third-party organizations.[30] Because he had the audacity to reveal this, Senator Fulbright was politically targeted by the American Zionists, who helped the Arkansas governor, Dale Bumpers, defeat Fulbright in 1974.

In the 1950s, in order to shore up the claim that the American Zionist Committee was a lobby (rather than an agent of Israel), Kenen and his organization were taken off the Jewish Agency payroll, domestic fundraising having reached the point of self-support. Also, a formal connection was made between the committee and the Conference of Presidents of Major American Jewish Organizations (Presidents' Conference for short). The problem was that the Presidents' Conference also took its foreign policy direction from Israel. Therefore, it comes as no surprise that both organizations maintained a significant connection with the Israeli ambassador.[31]

So close was the connection between the American Jewish/Zionist organizations and the Israeli government that, according to Edward Tivnan, "Jewish leaders rarely met with Administration officials without first being briefed by the [Israeli] embassy." William Waxler, who for two years served as the head of the Presidents' Conference, confessed to meeting with the Israeli ambassador almost weekly during his time in office. He also traveled to Israel "six to nine times a year" in order to "discuss tactics for Jewish support in the U.S." with Israeli government officials. As far as Waxler was concerned: "The American Jewish community has been used and should be used [by the Israeli government]. . . . Nobody is going off on their own and doing things without proper instructions. The only place where those instructions could really originate was in Israel." Under these circumstances, Israel's ambassador, Abba Eban, functioned as "the real head of the American Jewish community." And that community had become, in the words of an Israeli diplomat, "a spigot" that Israel could "turn on whenever it want[ed]."[32]

In the 1950s, the American Zionist Committee/AIPAC consolidated its influence over Congress. How this happened will be explained shortly, but even someone as independent minded as Secretary of State John Foster Dulles "openly asserted the difficulty of making foreign-policy decisions that displeased the organized Jewish community."[33] It was through Congress that pleasure or displeasure was most often registered. Influence with the executive branch of government in the post–World War II era first waxed, and then waned, and then waxed again. Zionist influence with Harry Truman was very strong, as his behavior in the lead-up to Israeli independence shows.[34] That influence waned when President Eisenhower (who, significantly, was not a professional politician) forced the Israelis to withdraw from Egypt's Sinai region following the 1956 British-French-Israeli invasion. Beginning with Presidents Kennedy and Johnson, Zionist influence waxed again and has remained substantial in the White House ever since.

There were many reasons for the post-Eisenhower growth in Zionist influence. After Eisenhower left office, the United States had a run of presidents who, for religious or cultural reasons, were fascinated with the Jews. Lyndon Baines Johnson is a good example. Claiming "my Christian faith sprang from yours," he would explain to American Jewish audiences "the similarities between the Jewish pioneers building a home in the desert [this is how he envisioned Palestine] and his own family's hardscrabble life farming . . . in the Hill Country of Texas." As it turned out, almost all the information Johnson ever got on the Middle East came not from his own country's State Department or intelligence services but from Israeli and American Zionist sources.[35]

However, probably more important in the long run for the growth in influence of the Zionist lobby was the fact that Jewish Americans became important donors to the political parties, particularly the Democrats. This gave their lobbying arms the necessary leverage to eventually convince the U.S. government to become Israel's principle financial and military supporter. The desire to compete for Jewish money brought the Republicans into range for the Zionists as well. And, after 1967 and the turning away from a liberal agenda by the American Jewish organizations, the Republican Party began to get Jewish financial backing. It was Richard Nixon, with his doctrine of reliance on allies to project American power around the world, who proclaimed that Israel was a "strategic asset."[36] The importance of money to the Israel lobby's effectiveness has been described by John Mearsheimer and Stephen Walt in their *The Israel Lobby and U.S. Foreign Policy*. As Mearsheimer and Walt tell us: "AIPAC's success is due to its ability to reward legislators and congressional can-

didates who support its agenda, and to punish those who challenge it.
. . . AIPAC makes sure its friends get strong financial support from the
myriad pro-Israel PACs. Those seen as hostile to Israel, on the other hand,
can be sure that AIPAC will direct campaign contributions to their political opponents."[37] To this may be added the fact that AIPAC often had
dynamic leadership, as in the case of Thomas Dine, who led the organization from 1980 to 1992. Under his guidance, a grassroots membership of
some fifty-five thousand was created, a staff of 150 hired, and an annual
budget of some $15 million established. The organization also managed
to become the chief source of information on Israel and related subjects
for most of the members of Congress. Thus, most of the talking points,
synopses, and research papers that inform ordinary congressmen and
senators about the sometimes esoteric issues, such as water rights, settlements, and borders, that concern the Israeli-Palestinian dispute as well as
the condition of Jews around the world come from AIPAC. In this way, it
has monopolized and continues to monopolize the information flow in
Israel's favor. To this end, AIPAC put together a small army of researchers
and writers to augment its team of lobbyists.[38]

The Problem of National Interests, Part 2

The 1970s showed the strength of the Israel lobby again and again. A
spectacular example of AIPAC's influence can be seen in the shaping of
U.S. foreign policy as regards the Soviet Union. The motivation, in terms
of the Jewish lobby, was Soviet Jewry, which appeared to be seeking to
emigrate in large numbers. Such an exodus would be a great demographic
boon to Israel, which has always feared the high birth rate of the Palestinians it sought to displace. Thus, the freedom of Jews to emigrate from
Russia became a high-priority issue for America's now very Zionist Jewish organizations. As was the case back in the late nineteenth century, the
pressure point used by the lobby was trade. In 1972, working with the
Washington State Democratic senator Henry Jackson (whose aide at the
time was the neoconservative Richard Perle), Zionist lobbyists such as
AIPAC's Isaiah Kenen helped prepare legislation that would deny the Soviet Union most-favored-nation status (which the Nixon administration
saw as an important step in its policy of detente) unless complete freedom
of emigration was allowed.[39]

It is to be noted that, at this time, the Soviet Union was not denying the Jews the right to emigrate. It was, however, using a quota system and levying a hefty exit tax (sometimes referred to as a *diploma tax*) on those who were highly educated. These policies are what had angered the Jewish American leadership. As in the case of the 1944 congressional resolutions, the political desire to comply with Zionist lobbying seemed to take precedence over what objective observers might have judged to be a number of national interests—detente with the Soviet Union, that nation's assistance in ending the Vietnam War, and the more peaceful world such steps potentially provided. The apparent sacrifice of national interests did not bother Richard Perle and other neoconservatives. Their ideology considered detente as but a dangerous illusion. Perle, on Jackson's behalf, worked to line up Democratic backing for the bill to deny trade status to the Soviets. Soon, he had seventy-two cosponsors in the Senate. So effective was this strategy that it moved the Soviets to drop the exit tax and promise to issue sixty thousand visas a year to Soviet Jews wanting to leave. In the end, the deal fell apart owing to extraneous events that neither the Nixon administration (then in the midst of the Watergate scandal) or the Jewish lobby organizations had anticipated.[40]

Nonetheless, the Jackson amendment (as the effort to deny the Soviet Union favored trade status became known) was seen as a great precedent by Zionist lobbyists. They felt that it had demonstrated the power of their lobby to force Congress, the executive branch, and even foreign governments to pay attention to their demands. This assumption was tested in the mid-1970s when Jewish organizations pushed for legislation that would outlaw compliance by U.S. businesses with the Arab embargo of Israel.

There were many factors that were involved in this demand. For instance, American companies did a lot of business with the Arab world, to say nothing of the fact that Middle East oil helped fuel much of the Western economy. Then there was the additional fact that the United States maintained its own embargoes against countries such as Cuba and Vietnam. As we saw in chapter 4, Congress would not hesitate to try to punish American and foreign firms for violations of these embargoes, just as the Arabs sought to blacklist American companies doing business with Israel. Nonetheless, when it came to the Arab embargo of Israel, Congress suddenly discovered a grave moral wrong.

Aided by representatives from AIPAC, legislation making cooperation with the Arab boycott a violation of U.S. law was introduced by Representative Jonathan Bingham of New York in early 1975. The debate that followed pitted the Jewish lobby against the Ford administration and representatives of big business. It turned out that the latter had some $4.5 billion at stake in Middle East business and was, thus, compelled to cooperate with the Arab boycott.[41] This level of investment demanded that some attempt at compromise be made, so, in the first half of 1976, a series of discussions were held between representatives of the major American Jewish organizations and the Business Roundtable (a lobby group that represented most of the country's big corporations). These were facilitated by the Carter White House. By May, legislation had been passed that reflected a compromise, some exceptions having been allowed in the antiboycott law, such as for the oil companies.

Once more, the Jewish lobby felt empowered. It had rewritten foreign policy. That the rescripting involved not a little hypocrisy and threatened a good amount of American foreign investment was never publicly noted. An objective observer might have pointed out that American government did to others what it was trying to punish the Arabs for doing. That observer might also have pointed out that a commonsense approach to national interest suggested that the nation protect its investments in the Arab world and maintain the goodwill of those who possessed the resources so necessary to the successful running of the economies of much of the West. But that is not how American politics worked. It was, once more, the parochial interests of those lobbies effective enough to influence the legislative process that stood in for national interests.

Even in those cases where the Jewish lobby had to accept compromise, or even when, owing to extraneous circumstances, it did not achieve its ends, it still ended up with an enhanced reputation for influence and power. A good example of such a case was the battle over the sale of airborne warning and command systems (AWACS) to Saudi Arabia in 1981.

The Saudis wished to buy five such spy planes from the United States largely as an early warning system guarding against attack from Iraq or Iran. However, the Israelis opposed the sale because, as they pointed out, the Saudis were technically still at war with Israel and might use the planes to warn against an Israeli attack. From a military standpoint, the Israelis had absolutely nothing to fear from the Saudi army or air force. However, the Saudis might have much more to fear from the Israelis. Saudi Arabia was among the most important suppliers of oil to the industrial world, so Washington had, arguably, a national interest in the defense of that nation from attack from any quarter. Nonetheless, Israel's position on the sale of AWACS demanded that the Jewish lobby fight wholeheartedly against it.

The sale was first backed by the Carter administration and then by Ronald Reagan (though Reagan had opposed it as long as he was campaigning for office against Carter). Once more, despite the reasonable national security arguments that could be made for the sale, the Congress was readily persuaded to stand against it by the effective lobbying of AIPAC and other Jewish groups. The House of Representatives voted on October 1, 1981, to reject the sale by a margin of 3–1.[42] The Senate was also set to turn the sale down. Under normal circumstances, Zionist parochial interests would have trumped national interest, dooming the sale. Then, on October 6, 1981, the president of Egypt, Anwar Sadat, was assassinated. All of a sudden, circumstances were no longer normal, and this one event proved enough to reverse congressional opinion. It now seemed that American allies in the Middle East were vulnerable to anti-American and anti-Israeli forces both external and internal. It was this fear that allowed the sale to go through.

The Suppression of Free Speech for American Jewry

Despite losing this specific battle because of the unexpected assassination of an American ally, the increasingly right-wing Jewish organizational leadership became ever more effective in influencing U.S. foreign policy. The Zionist lobby continued to work closely with the administration of Ronald Reagan. Reagan's admiration for Israel and its role in the region flowed primarily from his Christian fundamentalist outlook. Also, ideologically, the Jewish neoconservatives fit in well with Reagan's hard-line approach to the cold war world. It was this president who swapped detente for stigmatizing the Soviet Union as the "evil empire." In Israel, a corresponding ideological turn to the right had occurred when, in 1977, Israeli voters brought to power Menachem Begin and his Likud Party.[43] The Jewish American neoconservatives quickly became close advisers to the Likud government in Jerusalem.

It was also around this time that AIPAC came to the fore as the enforcement arm of the Conference of Presidents of Major American Jewish Organizations. As mentioned above, AIPAC had developed a symbiotic relationship with the Presidents' Conference. The two organizations had interlocking directorates. The chair of the Presidents' Conference was always a member of the inner ruling body (sometimes known as the *officers' group*) of AIPAC. As J. J. Goldberg tells it: "The job of the Presidents' Conference was to forge a consensus on Israel from among the diverse views of organized American Jews. Translating those views into political clout was the job of AIPAC."[44] This relationship becomes suspect, however, when it is realized that the foreign policy positions taken by the Presidents' Conference were often dictated by the Israeli government.[45] When it came to influencing American Middle East policy, that made the Presidents' Conference, and AIPAC, de facto agents of a foreign power. In the case of AIPAC, this has even involved charges of espionage on Israel's behalf.[46]

It is a curious aspect of the story of the transformation of these powerful American Jewish organizations into arms of the Israeli government that the main argument in this process was the sanctity of Israeli democracy. Those who argued against the right of American Jews to be publicly critical of Israel insisted that, as Goldberg put it, "Israelis were the only ones entitled to decide Israeli policy, since they alone bore the risks." The job of American Jews was to "stand publically united with Israel." And, since, for instance, it was the Israeli decision not to negotiate with the Palestinians because, allegedly, they were all terrorists, American Jews were forbidden to urge otherwise. This was the official position of the Presidents' Conference and AIPAC.[47] In other words, American Jews were told that, in order to respect Israeli democracy, they must forgo their right to free speech on the subject of Israel. Throwing a bone to the disappointed, the increasingly undemocratic American Jewish leadership said that it was all right for Jews to air their differences in private. However, public disagreement with the official line meant effective ostracization from the Jewish community.

A case in point is the short history of the small progressive American Jewish organization known as Breira (the word *breira* means "alternative" in Hebrew). Breira was founded in 1973, and its membership never numbered more than fifteen hundred nationwide. Most of its members were intellectuals and young liberal rabbis. What they sought to do was promote a discussion on the topic of what was the proper relationship between diaspora Jews and Israel. After the Yom Kippur War, the organization took a public position urging mutual recognition between Israel and the Palestinians. Although the members of Breira were too few in number to mount a serious challenge to the likes of the Presidents' Conference and AIPAC, these and other major Jewish organizations went after them as if they were traitors. They were condemned by all the leaders of organized Jewry from Reform through Orthodox Judaism. Establishment leaders would not appear at events if a Breira member was also on the agenda. Breira members were also castigated by Israeli diplomats in the United States and, ultimately, accused of "giving aid and comfort . . . to those who would cut aid to Israel and leave it defenseless before murderers and terrorists."[48] These tactics, which the American Jewish writer Irving Howe called "heimishe [homebred] witch hunting,"[49] were similar to those used by the Soviet Comintern to maintain discipline among "diaspora" Communists in the 1920s and 1930s. And, as with dissenting Communists, the tactics worked when it came to the Jews of America. Breira was defunct by 1977.

Breira met its fate while Israel was governed by the Labor Party. In 1977, things would get much worse for independent-minded American Jews. In that year, Menachem Begin took the reigns of power in Israel. When Begin was elected prime minister of Israel, the chair of the Presidents' Conference in the United States was Alexander Schindler, the leader of Reform Jewry in America. Schindler was a liberal in all things but Israel. After going to Israel to meet Begin personally, he became convinced that American Jewry must accept and follow the prime minister because he was democratically elected and because he appeared to "really care" about American Jews. Thus, Schindler manipulated and prodded most of American Jewry into defending policies of imperialist expansion instituted by the Likud government.[50] A year later, with American Jewish discomfort with Israeli settlement policies growing at the community level, the Israelis brought eight leaders of major American organizations to Israel. For three days, they had long meetings with Begin, Defense Minister Ezer Weizman, and Foreign Minister Moshe Dayan. They were given helicopter tours of the West Bank and generally lectured on why the Israeli government could not possibly trade land for peace. They went home staunch supporters of Menachem Begin.

Simultaneously, the Israeli government started to concentrate its influence on the Presidents' Conference and AIPAC. Other Jewish organizations, such as the long-established National Jewish Community Relations Advisory Council, were increasingly ignored by the Israelis. It was assumed that the Presidents' Conference and AIPAC would discipline such organizations, forcing them to toe the Israeli propaganda line. The Israelis had made this strategic decision because AIPAC had proved itself increasingly able to penetrate the policy-formulating ranks of the American government. For example, following the AWACS vote in 1981, a vote that the Zionist lobbyists had actually lost, the Reagan administration had made a decision to enlist AIPAC as an ally rather than an opponent. To this end, administration officials approached AIPAC to participate in the government's Middle East policy-formulation process.[51] At the same time, anyone within the foreign policy bureaucracy who was critical of the evolving U.S. alliance with Israel was pushed out of the policymaking process. Congress saw no problem in this arrangement, for its members had long ago come to regularly consult the Israeli lobby on pending relevant legislation. In 1983, the Reagan administration solicited a "formal strategic alliance" with Israel, the overture resulting in the signing of a "memorandum of understanding on strategic cooperation." By 1987, Israel was designated a "major non-Nato ally," a status that gave it access to most U.S. military technology.[52]

It was AIPAC's reputation for influence in Congress that convinced the Reagan officials that these were smart moves. The Reagan people should have known of AIPAC's connection to the Israeli government—certainly, the American intelligence agencies did. It apparently made no difference, particularly to a president who had a biblically inspired admiration for the Israelis. In any case, by 1983, Israel was a formal military partner of the United States. The two governments would now mutually engage in such adventures as "aiding the Nicaraguan contras, training security forces in Zaire, sending arms secretly to Iran," and more. The "sharing of technology and information and intelligence reached unprecedented proportions."[53] When Begin sent the Israeli army into Lebanon in June 1982 and ended up shelling Beirut and allowing massacres of Palestinians at the Shabra and Shatilla camps, the operations were conducted, in part, with American weapons. Reagan, who feebly protested this usage to Begin (it is against U.S. law for foreign nations to use American military aid for offensive purposes), was momentarily regarded by the prime minister as a hostile gentile.

As has been noted, many American Jews found the behavior of Israel in the occupied territories and in Lebanon very unsettling. Polls taken at the time show that nearly two-thirds of American Jews were "troubled" by Israeli policies. Yet, in practice, individual American Jews looked the other way and literally took refuge in their localism. Not willing to turn opinion into organized action, this majority abdicated to the minority of American Jews who were willing and able to act in an organized and national way. Polls also show that 70 percent of Jewish leaders at the community level were also "troubled" but went along with the national dictates so as to maintain their positions of local leadership.[54] For his part, Menachim Begin proved not as concerned about the feelings of American Jews as Schindler and others had believed. He simply ignored them. His Likud Party successor, the old terrorist Yitzhak Shamir, was interested in American Jews only to the extent that he could turn them into, as Goldberg puts it, "an organ of Likud policy." To this end, the Presidents' Conference and AIPAC were brought into the inner circles of Likud politics. So compromised were the leadership positions of these American organizations that the Israeli government considered them as equivalent to "any top ambassadorial or civil service job."[55] Given that the Israeli government was now very right-wing, it should come as no surprise that it saw to it that neoconservative American Jewish leaders such as Morris B. Abram (who headed what passed for a civil rights commission in the Reagan administration) became the chair of the Presidents' Conference and a mouthpiece for Likud views.

Those who were seen as critical in any way whatsoever, even though they had otherwise proved themselves loyal to the Israeli cause, were castigated as traitors and intimidated into silence. Take the case of Senator Frank Lautenberg, the Jewish senator from New Jersey who had both served as the chairman of the United Jewish Appeal and helped smooth the way for Russian Jewish emigration. However, in 1987, he made the mistake of initiating a letter commending Secretary of State George Shultz for his efforts at seeking a compromise settlement of the Arab-Israeli conflict. Prime Minister Shamir took exception to this gesture, and almost immediately Zionist Americans from across Lautenberg's state started to attack him and work against his reelection. "What I saw was almost a venomous response," the senator said. "Suddenly I was painted a pariah." Lautenberg, who remarked that he had commended Shultz because he thought a compromise peace was in the best interest of the United States (as well as Israel), observed: "I was shocked by the response from some segments of the Jewish community. I was practically accused of being a traitor to the cause."[56]

American Jewish intellectuals supportive of the Labor Party element in Israeli politics could find a home at the Washington Institute for Near Eastern Policy (WINEP). WINEP was established in 1984 by Larry Weinberg, a past president of AIPAC, and its first director was Martin Indyk, who had once been the research director at AIPAC. The institute saw its goal as "moving beltway [Washington, DC] thinking toward Israel" and, thereby, making it possible for the U.S. government to "resist the pressures for a procedural breakthrough [on Palestinian-Israeli peace issues] until conditions have ripened."[57] In other words, WINEP sought to make it possible for the U.S. government to resist peace while Israel continued to expand its illegal colonies, thus creating facts on the ground that would, in the long run, preclude the possibility of an independent Palestinian state. With this as a goal, it made little difference that the institute was controlled by people more aligned with Israel's Labor Party than with Likud. When it came to expansion and the occupation of Palestinian land, the difference between the two Israeli parties, though sometimes bitterly expressed, was, ultimately, tactical. And, in any case, no matter which party was in power, all important positions taken by the Presidents' Conference and AIPAC referencing the Middle East were carefully aligned with those taken by the reigning Israeli government.[58]

As suggested above, the ordinary individuals who made up the American Jewish community, once so noted for its progressive and liberal attitudes, simply acquiesced in this situation. In part, this was due to ignorance. As one observer put it, many Jews "don't have a strong sense of just how precisely their community is being defined daily by their capital lobbyists."[59] Another part of the explanation is the historically conditioned acceptance of the argument that all Jews must maintain a united front when it comes to Israel. Both these reactions fit well with the notion that American Jews generally live according to the theory of localism put forth in the first chapter of this book. Of course, a good number of them are influenced by issues of ethnic identity. For the more attentive, this makes Israel a virtual component of their local environment. Yet it must be borne in mind that the news about Israel and the Middle East is brought to them through a largely self-censoring media, as well as through the pulpits of their rabbis and the offices of their organizational leaders. Most of these sources are less than objective and do not encourage individual analysis and debate. Thus, American Jews (like most of the rest of the people in the United States and beyond) live in an information environment that shapes and skews their perceptions and reactions.

Conclusion

AIPAC supporters will often say that what they are doing is practicing the right of all American citizens to petition their government and hold their representatives accountable for their actions. And, not only do they do this effectively and efficiently in Washington, DC, but they also have "members active in the camp of nearly every candidate for every seat in Congress."[60] There is, on the face of it, nothing illegal about any of this. This is, one might way, the way the system works. However, when an organization of such influence most often takes its cue from a foreign state rather than from the democratically debated and decided desires of a community of American citizens it claims to represent, then the right-to-petition argument becomes highly questionable. Yet the same influence over policy that makes AIPAC and its allied American Jewish lobbies so powerful has saved it from being labeled an operative of a foreign government and made to register as such.[61]

A good example of the consequences of this arrangement was the role played by the Israel lobby in promoting the Second Iraq War. In *The Israel Lobby and U.S. Foreign Policy*, Mearsheimer and Walt dedicated thirty-three pages and 175 footnotes to documenting the link between the Zionist lobby and the invasion of Iraq. The lobby's prowar position was taken because, by late 2002, the Israeli government had decided to back war with Iraq.[62] Mearsheimer and Walt conclude that both Israel and its lobby "played crucial roles in making [the invasion of Iraq] happen" and that, without their pressure, the invasion would "almost certainly not have occurred."[63]

There are knowledgeable observers who say that Mearsheimer and Walt give too much credit to the Israel lobby when it comes to shaping

policy. Such critics would most likely also take issue with the whole notion of privatizing foreign policy. In particular, Noam Chomsky, the notable critic of American foreign policy from the Massachusetts Institute
of Technology, and Joseph Massad, from Columbia University, have both
asserted that the Mearsheimer and Walt thesis denies structural interests
that shape American policy worldwide and not just in the Middle East.
Chomsky describes these structural interests as "strategic-economic interests of concentrations of domestic power in the tight state-corporate
linkage."[64] The Chomsky-Massad position is that these interests stand
prior to any special interests, which, in terms of foreign policy, gain influence only to the extent that their parochial interests serve to further the
structural national interests of the state. Thus, the lobby power and the
privatization positions are seen as reductionist. In Massad's words, they
"exonerate the United States government from all responsibility and guilt
that it deserves."[65] While experts can differ as to just what the distribution
of influence is among "concentrations of domestic power" at any one time
or relative to any particular foreign policy, the fact remains that such concentrations of power are, at bottom, special interests. Chomsky lists some
of them—"oil companies, arms industries and other special interests . . ."
—in the very piece in which he takes issue with Walt and Mearsheimer. It
would seem that, structurally conceived or not, there is no foreign policy
formulation for the Middle East apart from special interests. One cannot make a sharp distinction between the "responsibility and guilt" of the
U.S. government and of the special interests that effectively influence the
behavior of that government.

To the extent that the Israel lobby did influence the decision to invade
Iraq, it did so without any prior extended debate or popular feedback
from the American Jewish community it claims to represent. Did any of
the lobby's myriad volunteers note this lack of democratic procedure? Or,
like good soldiers, do they find it quite normal that AIPAC decisions are
made behind closed doors by a relatively small officers' group that just
happens to have periodic meetings with Israeli diplomats and officials?
The troops of the Israel lobby (as of 2006, AIPAC claimed to have 100,000
members) are simply given their marching orders, and, glorying in being
associated with such a powerful and influential organization, off they go.
Yet what are the consequences of this situation for the defining of U.S.
national interests in the Middle East? Our unnaturally close relationship

with Israel has, at the very least, helped bring the reputation of the United States to a very low state and, simultaneously, abetted the growth of anti-American movements in the region.

A rational outside observer, standing above the influence of special interests, however configured, would not have too much difficulty figuring out what American national interests are in the Middle East. First and foremost, American interest lies in the maintenance of a peaceful, stable, and pro-American regional environment that assures uninterrupted access to necessary resources such as oil at reasonable, fair market rates as well as in the carrying on of other commercial and cultural activities of mutual benefit. Overt or covert policies that erode pro-American feelings by identifying the United States with dictatorial regimes or apartheid-style behavior can and do lead to hostile actions, such as attacks on American tourists, businesses, embassies, and consulates and also such attacks as occurred on September 11, 2001. Such policies are obviously counterproductive. It is in the national interest that they be avoided and that a policy of noncooperation be adopted toward countries whose governments pursue policies that complicate or make difficult the maintenance of such a regionally stable and friendly environment.

No country in the Middle East, be it Iran, Syria, Libya, or Iraq, has made the region more dangerous and difficult for American interests than Israel. Here is why. First, the immense influence and obstructionist tactics of organizations and lobbyists whose first loyalty is to Israel have made it nearly impossible for the United States to respond to Israeli behavior that undermines a stable and pro-American environment in that region. Second, almost every peace initiative offered by U.S. administrations over the past forty years has been actively or passively rejected by Israel. Yet the Congress and the executive branch have repeatedly been unable to adequately respond and discipline Israel because of the power of the Israel lobby. Third, the lobby also sees to it that Israel drains resources from the U.S. Treasury to fund activities that are not only against U.S. interest (because they stir up hatred against America) but in violation of international law (e.g., settlement activities and the building of the misnamed security wall). Fourth, the United States has repeatedly been induced by lobby power to diplomatically protect Israel from UN condemnation through the use of its Security Council veto. In doing so, it once more publicly ties itself to Israeli policies and, thereby, declares its complicity in that country's often illegal and violent behavior. Fifth, as a consequence, access to the Middle East for U.S. businesses, tourism, cultural endeavors, and the like has been increasingly difficult and dangerous. One historian of the issue has estimated that, as a consequence, "American companies and the United States economy suffer an estimated $1 billion loss per year."[66] Sixth, Islamic fundamentalists, of both the violent and the nonviolent variety, have had a field day quite accurately associating our support of Israel with the suffering of the Palestinians. Seventh, Israel has repeatedly ignored the limitations placed by law on the use of the military equipment given to it by the United States. It has, at one time or another, used such equipment repeatedly in an illegal offensive manner against all its neighbors. Thus, Palestinian, Lebanese, Syrian, Jordanian, and Egyptian civilians have, because of Israeli actions, been killed or maimed by ordinance "made in the USA." Because of the power of the Israeli lobby, Israel suffers no consequences for such violations, but American interests are harmed irreparably. Arguably, the attack of September 11, 2001, is, to date, the most profound proof that support of Israel has brought nothing but disaster for U.S. interests. Yet, owing to the inordinate power of this particular special interest faction, policies in direct contravention of American national interests in the Middle East continue to be pursued.

6

Is There a National Interest?

The evidence and examples given so far suggest that the notion of a national interest is at best problematic. Certainly, well-organized interest groups with strong feelings about how American foreign policy should operate in a particular part of the world can and often do shape government actions. In this way, they effectively privatize foreign policy relative to their areas of interest. Their parochial interest becomes the so-called national interest.

Nonetheless, there is truly a vast American literature dealing with the topic of how Americans should conceive of and pursue their national interest. Authors ranging from Alexis de Tocqueville to Samuel Huntington have written on the subject, and there is still an ongoing debate as to how the subject should be understood. Much of the literature, though not all, organizes itself around a number of schools of thought. These constitute theoretical approaches to the subject of national interest and work on the assumption that it is a real phenomenon, shaping the international relations not only of the United States but of all states. Thus, before we can draw any definitive conclusions about national interest, we must consider these arguments.

The School of the Realists

Realists of various shades want a foreign policy that accords with the facts of human nature as it has supposedly manifested itself through the ages. According to the realists, it is a basic fact of human nature that, over the long run, people act according to their interests and levels of power.[1] Working from this assumption, the realists then assign this same nature to the state. That is, they anthropomorphize the state, giving it the behavioral characteristics of an amoral human being. The anthropomorphized state is amoral because it acts in a realm without a uniformly applicable and enforceable code of law. Just like an individual, the state has (national) interests that, in realist terms, are defined as military and economic security. According to Hans J. Morgenthau, one of the primary spokesmen for the classical realist school, the assumption that statesmen (acting as representatives of the state) pursue the national interest gives some predictability to the behavior of states. It also makes possible a theoretical understanding of international politics. Thus, political leaders addressing foreign policy will act according to national interest regardless of ideology, religion, or the nature of their governments. This is because, when it is rational, their behavior is, according to Morgenthau, dictated by the a priori structural nature of the essentially lawless international relations system.[2] It is only by recognizing that such a realist sense of national interest exists, and is ubiquitous among nation-states, that statesmen can "speak the same language—that of interest—and achieve common ground for compromise" (as in the case of treaties).[3]

National leaders run into trouble when they start confusing the desirable with the possible, that is, when they confuse their own biased view of what is achievable with a hardheaded and realistic analysis of what is possible. This, the realists assert, is a particular danger within democratic societies. For it is in environments where the politician is called on to be responsive to the citizenry that, as David Clinton puts it, the "contingent elements of personality, prejudice, and subjective preferences, and the weaknesses of intellect, . . . are bound to deflect foreign policies from their rational course."[4] In other words, it is harder to secure military and economic security if one has to take into account the desires of a multitude of individual and group interests. Another risk, found not just in the democratic milieu, is what Morgenthau calls the "replacement of experience with superstition" owing to the "egotism of the policy makers." Or, if you will, the leader's failure to adjust his or her "picture of the world in the light of experience . . . and the use of intelligence for the purpose not of adapting policy to reality, but of reinterpreting reality to fit policy."[5] Here, policymakers, buffeted by the emotions of the crowd and/or their own subjective biases, leave the rational and realist path of national interest–driven policy.

It is interesting to find Morgenthau citing the Vietnam War (he calls it "the war in Indo-China") as an example of the latter predicament. American policy during that war, he suggests, ended up deviating from a rational assessment of what was possible in terms of U.S. policy and started to reflect "the personal whim or personal psychopathology of the policy maker." This was seen in President Johnson's inability to retreat and the decision to just keep pouring in troops as the American quagmire deepened. It was also reflected in President Nixon's insistence on "peace with honor" through an expansion of the war into Cambodia and Laos. Morgenthau believes that the inability to recognize and respect the difference between what is possible and the policymaker's "personal wish" is a form of policy-distorting pathology.[6] However, the possibility that the realists do not consider is that there may very well be no understanding of national interests apart from the biased interests of leaders and interest groups. If that is so, the pathology that Morgenthau describes must always afflict all the players in the game of international relations. As a general rule, it is not reality that motivates any of us. Rather, it is what we think is real. *Pathology unavoidable ?*

The realists are also suspicious of the demand that "universal moral principles be applied to the actions of states." Morgenthau insists that, in terms of state action, morality must be "filtered through the concrete circumstances of time and place" and, therefore, is independent of universal morals. The only "moral principle" that can really motivate state action is "national survival."[7] George Kennan, also of the realist school, would agree. In his influential *American Diplomacy, 1900–1950,* Kennan complains that American foreign policy has traditionally been burdened by "a legalistic-moralistic approach to international problems." He defined this approach as "the belief that it should be possible to suppress the chaotic and dangerous aspirations of governments in the international field by the acceptance of some system of legal rules and restraints." He thinks that this assumption is dangerously naive and prevents us from dealing with "awkward conflicts on their merits with a view to finding the solutions least unsettling to the stability of international life."[8] A proper realistic approach to international affairs would be pragmatic and clearheaded and isolated from the emotionalism of public opinion.

Kennan's and Morgenthau's approach presents a problem for national leaders in a country like the United States where, according to the realist international relations scholar John Mearsheimer, American voters see their nation as the most highly principled one in the entire world. The citizens of the United States see themselves as moral and principled, and they want their country to reflect that self-image. Mearsheimer explains that American leaders finesse this contradiction by the use of "spin doctors" who "tell a story to the American people that makes it look like what the United States is doing is completely consistent with its ideals."[9] Realists, however, will recognize as mere propaganda this spin as well as the almost universal tactic of state leaders to clothe their own particular aspirations and actions in, as Morgenthau puts it, "the moral purposes of the universe," that is, the "blasphemous" claim that "God is always on one's side." In the end, the United States, like all other nation-states, should act by "weighing . . . the consequences of alternative political actions" in terms of how they might affect the "power of the nation" and its "national interests."[10] In classical terms, the nation should practice realpolitik.

As Michael H. Hunt tells us, Kennan and other classical realists "nursed a deep faith that detached, coolly analytic experts, sitting around committee tables in the Pentagon, the State Department, and the White House, could in their collective wisdom grasp the realities of international affairs."[11] However, what happens to this proposition if, in fact, such experts must take direction from leaders who pursue their biased parochial interests or those of their interest group supporters? In that case, the realist insistence that international relations are governed by state survival and the maximization of state power becomes a cover for the use of state institutions to achieve private interests.

There are many variations on the theme of realism in international relations. The classical realists, of whom Morgenthau and Kennan are representatives, were followed by a school of neorealists or structural realists. The main representative here is Kenneth Waltz. Waltz deemphasizes the individual actor or national leader in international relations and emphasizes the structural nature of the international state system. Where the classical realists see national leaders and their desire to assure national survival as reflecting an anarchic world, the neorealists assert that the very nature of the nation-state system creates structure. And it is within the parameters of that structure that successful states restrict their behav-

You would have to have Mannheim's free-floating intellectuals.

esp. Mearsheimer

ior. Nonetheless, "in the absence of a supreme authority," there is always the possibility of military conflict, and that drives all states to plan for the worst-case scenario of armed conflict.[12] Neorealists, in turn, have been followed by postclassical realists, who provide a wider range of consequences for the drive for maximum power among states. The classical realist would say that the drive for power reflects a drive for domination and, ultimately, conquest. The postclassical realists factor in the drive for economic resources and insist that part of the behavior shaping the structure of international relations is the constant taking of cost-benefit analyses as a guide to action. This makes states considerably more cautious than they might otherwise appear in the classical and neorealist versions of realist theory.[13]

Whatever brand of realism you prefer, the assumption underlying them all is deterministic. Somehow, ideally, the state and the structure of international relations can break loose from, and stand independently of, the personalities that collectively make it real. The very possibility that the drive for power and survival can be captured by special interest factions that reshape the concept of national interest in private terms is deemed a corrupting pathology. To have the system of international relations work correctly, in a smooth and predictable way, national leaders and their foreign office bureaucrats and diplomats must suspend all biases and personal interests and allow themselves to be driven, consciously or unconsciously, to seek power and, often, to act violently by the pure motives of national security and survival. At best, this can be structured by the set nature of the international system. This is the realist party line. But do human beings act in such a fashion?

The School of the Idealists

Idealists are the polar opposite of realists when it comes to the assumptions made about human nature and its impact on international relations. They view people as normally good rather than bad. Conflict is not an inherent or natural part of international interaction, and, thus, it is not inevitable. Rather, peace is broadly recognized as preferable and achievable. Ethical standards of behavior are applicable to international relations, and foreign policy should be used to spread the concepts of democracy, human rights, and the like. International laws that try to promote ethical behavior, such as the Geneva Conventions, should be supported, and, to this end, international organizations such as the United Nations and the International Criminal Court should be strengthened. Collective security is the only real security in terms of international relations. It is to be noted here that the basic aspect of national interest—the achieving of military and economic security—is the same for both realists and idealists. It is the strategy and tactics for achieving that goal that are qualitatively different.

While many realists see the idealists as hopelessly naive, this is really not the case. Idealists know that it is not the job of statesmen to manufacture a utopia. They insist instead that, where possible, foreign policy push the envelope when it comes to promoting decent behavior in the world. And, according to a recent poll carried out by the Pew Research Center, some 72 percent of Americans believe that moral principles should "be a top priority in the way the U.S. conducts foreign policy."[14] The limitations of such polls must, of course, be borne in mind. That people voice such opinions does not mean that they routinely pay much attention to foreign policy. However, when confronted with the question of the behavior of nation-states, they extrapolate from the ideal for interpersonal relations. It is a projection of localism into the realm of international relations.

The idealist school does not have the same number of famous theorists as does the realist school. However, it does have notable models in terms of past American national leaders. For instance, both Woodrow Wilson and Jimmy Carter are seen as past presidents of note in the idealist vein. However, when it comes to an examination of the actual policies pursued by these idealist presidents, what is often found is an array of mixed messages.

Wilson (who served as president from 1913 to 1921), for example, brought the United States into World War I with the rhetorical claims that it was a war to uphold civilization and that victory would spread democracy. There is no reason to doubt that he actually believed his own words. It is true that there was a partial, and temporary, spread of democracy into Eastern Europe as the defeated empires of Germany, Austria, and Russia crumbled. On the other hand, democracy was denied the peoples in the colonies of these defeated nations as well as those of the Ottoman Empire. In these non-European areas, self-determination was withheld because of the alleged political immaturity of the inhabitants. As a consequence, these areas were handed over to the less than tender care of the victorious empires of Britain and France under the guise of a "mandate system." This was a demand of Wilson's allies and the price he had to pay for their support of the League of Nations. Wilson, an American Southerner with racially biased views of nonwhites, went along with the deal without much protest.[15]

Wilson put a lot of stock in the establishment of the League of Nations as an embodiment of international law. He felt that whatever imperfections there were in the Paris peace treaty that ended World War I could be corrected for over time through the workings of the league.[16] These hopes did not work out, and the flaws of the Paris settlement quickly led to a renewed breakdown of international order in Europe that also killed off the League of Nations. Whether this all happened because, as the realists would claim, human nature naturally tends toward conflict or because a draconian peace treaty, compounded by the Great Depression, pushed half the world into accepting authoritarian rulers who promised prosperity and glory through the reassertion of militarism is still debated.

As for Jimmy Carter (president from 1977 to 1981), he has generally been accused by American conservatives as well as foreign policy realists of being naive and not understanding how foreign policy worked. These charges are both untrue and unfair. As president, Carter grasped the nature of international situations confronting him very quickly. He had come to office promising to promote human rights as well as related goals such as arms control and, wherever possible, reconciliation with adversaries. Early in his administration, he signed several international human rights accords and expanded the human rights bureau of the State Department. According to James Fallows, who was one of his speechwriters, Carter was very careful with his rhetoric on the topic of human rights: "He was not saying this was the only lodestone of our policy [or that] we could impose it everywhere, but that on balance we would stand for it. That we've recognized complications but we'd always push for this as a goal."[17]

Inevitably, the Carter administration ran into contradictions and had to prioritize its goals. For example, when it came to relations with the Soviet Union, there were multiple ends. Among them were arms control, nuclear nonproliferation, and human rights issues such as the emigration of ethnic minorities and the treatment of dissidents such as Andrei Sakharov. The Soviets were not going to cooperate on the former if they were pressed too hard on the latter (which they considered internal affairs). Here is an example of where idealism met realism, and the difficulties of finessing these issues were interpreted by Carter's foes as signs of ineptness.[18] In truth, the only answer the realists had for this dilemma was to drop the issue of human rights altogether.

It would seem at first glance that the idealists would be more susceptible to the demands of those special interest groups that seek to privatize foreign policy. For instance, Zionist groups in the United States made a major issue of emigration restrictions on Jews seeking to leave the Soviet Union for Israel. Cuban special interests in the United States make an issue of those seeking to leave Castro's Cuba. This sort of issue is of particular appeal to domestic ethnic groups whose fellows are residing in countries that are unfriendly to the United States. In truth, both the idealist and the realist camps are equally susceptible to interest groups, but their susceptibility varies with the nature of the lobby. For instance, the demands of the arms industry and oil conglomerates are likely to have more of an impact on realist politicians than are those of human rights groups, which in turn would more likely have the ear of idealist politicians. The idealists share one other important point in common with the realists. They too anthropomorphize the state and speak of nations as if they were individuals with interests that stand above and independent from the private interests of competing groups of citizens.

The School of the Neoconservatives

There are other schools purporting to have powerful analyses of just what the national interest is and how best to realize it. In chapter 3, the character and intent of the neoconservatives were touched on. They too are considered to represent a school of thought when it comes to international relations. Some observers see them as a hybrid of idealism and realism—their goal being a kind of Wilsonian benevolent American hegemony but without any reliance on international organizations. Matthew Yglesias, writing in the *Atlantic,* explains that neoconservatives may want to benefit the world by bringing it democracy. However, they want democracy delivered as a part of American hegemony within a unipolar political world. He points out that neocons such as William Kristol and Robert Kagan believe that America's "clear moral purpose" and its "fundamental

national interests" are always in harmony.[19] President George W. Bush has
bought into this, declaring in his second inaugural address: "America's vital interests and our deepest beliefs are now one."[20] Thus, for the neoconservatives and those influenced by them, it would seem that the United
States can realize its national interests of military and economic security
only by reshaping the world in its own image. And, they assert, this is not
only good for America; it is also good for the world.

The neoconservatives treat their strategic vision as if it had divine
sanction. If there is a problem, it is tactical—how best to realize this unipolar world. The current generation of neocons has concluded that, as
Yglesias puts it, the United States "isn't being as forceful as it needs to be
in asserting and reasserting its hegemonic position." After all, with the
Soviet Union gone, this is the historical moment for the United States
to realize its destiny. So what happens when, in reality, George W. Bush's
neoconservative administration meets up with contradictions similar
to those faced by the Carter administration? For instance, how to deal
with the claim that we are spreading democracy in parts of the world
where free and fair elections would almost certainly bring to power anti-
American governments? It would seem that the neoconservative answer
is to assert ever more military force. The contradictions will go away once
we control the world. Yglesias sees this neoconservative position as not
so much insincere as "intellectually shoddy." What it has resulted in is "a
kind of mindless militarism."[21]

Some of the neoconservatives feel that such an analysis oversimpli
fies their positions. Charles Krauthammer, the neoconservative editorial
writer, insists that there are actually two different neoconservative visions
for foreign policy and the national interest: "There is the democratic globalism advocated by Blair and Bush and elaborated by such thinkers as
Robert Kagan and Bill Kristol. And there is the democratic realism I have
long advocated. Both are 'democratic' because they advocate the spread
of democracy as both an end and a means of American foreign policy.
But one is 'realism' because it rejects the universalistic scope and high
idealism of democratic globalism."[22] In other words, Krauthammer feels
that the United States should restructure only parts of the world, not all
of it—which makes the difference between the two sorts of neoconservatives more quantitative than qualitative. Also, which parts get restructured
should be decided on the basis of a realist criterion of strategic necessity.

For Krauthammer, the first and foremost part of the globe that needs re-structuring is the Middle East because it is the home region of America's strategic enemy, Arab/Islamic radicalism.

I suggested in chapter 3 that the neoconservatives constitute a lobby, or special interest, that has succeeded in capturing important aspects of foreign policy formulation, thus essentially privatizing that process to serve its parochial interests. Others have also described the neoconservatives as a special interest group. In *America Alone*, Stefan Halper and Jonathan Clarke tell us that neoconservatism has as "a special interest focused on its particular agenda" and, thereby, "taken American international relations on an unfortunate detour, veering away from . . . traditional Republican internationalism." They admit that the neoconservatives are not a "card-carrying organization."[23] (Irving Kristol has described neoconservatism as "a persuasion.")[24] However, they insist that they meet the basic definition of a lobby as an organized minority, "sharing identifiable characteristics and similar concerns" that are forcefully advocated to affect policy.[25]

Halper and Clarke, critiquing neoconservatism from a moderate Republican position, make the following additional observations. First, the neoconservative talk about "freedom, democracy and human rights" (i.e., about the stuff of American foreign policy idealism) is "largely rhetorical." Anyone who knows anything about the Muslim world must agree with this assessment. For, as noted above, it is strikingly obvious that, if democracy in the form of free and fair elections were practiced just about anywhere in that region, the result would almost certainly be a government hostile to the United States. However, Halper and Clarke tell us that, in truth, the neoconservatives really believe that it is a winner-take-all, kill-or-be-killed world "where perpetual militarized competition for ascendency is the norm." It is this sort of contradiction that leads to the blackmail situation faced by the Palestinians after the victory of Hamas. You can vote for whomever you want in your fair and free national election, but, if you elect the wrong party, we will slap draconian sanctions on you. Second, while the long-range goal of the neocons is certainly global unipolar hegemony, their present focus is almost obsessively on the Middle East. Halper and Clarke note that 80 percent of *Present Dangers*, a collection of essays edited by Robert Kagan and William Kristol constituting a "neoconservative canon," focuses on the Middle East.[26]

R. Kagan

Why are the neoconservatives so fixated on the Middle East? Well, they certainly seem to be great believers in the proposition of a clash of civilizations. And the enemy civilization for every neoconservative out there is Islam. Krauthammer describes the "threat" from the Arab/Islamic world as an "existential" one.[27] It is not a coincidence that the Israelis use the same term for the same threat. In the neoconservative universe, Israel is our most loyal and useful ally, not just in the Middle East, but globally. Ever since the Reagan administration, the Israelis have been involved in covert actions with the United States in places as far afield as Central America. Israeli defense industries are now intertwined with American ones, and Israelis have been brought in to assist the U.S. Homeland Security Agency. Indeed, for the neoconservatives, Israel is the very model of an aggressive state seeking to maximize its power and resources in a Hobbesian environment. The neocons want the United States to behave like Israel.[28]

Thus, the neoconservative "persuasion" is really not a hybrid of realism and idealism. It is, rather, a radical distortion of elements of both these schools. The neocons share with the realists a pessimistic view of human nature and the belief that conflict is inherent in the international state system. To this they melodramatically add the assertion that life is a battle between good and evil. Many neoconservatives point to World War II and the Nazi-bred Holocaust to prove their point. One might counter that, historically, there have been periods of peace and periods of war. Why the warlike behavior should characterize human nature any more than the peaceful behavior is hard to know. The realists and the neocons simply prioritize the former. Having made their choice, the neocons specifically seem to feel themselves liberated to act aggressively because that is human nature. On the other hand, realists such as Hans Morgenthau and George Kennan certainly would not support the policies of the George W. Bush administration. They would not advocate the outright distortion of intelligence, the invasion of another country based on deception, and the unnecessary alienation of traditional allies. Indeed, there is very little doubt that Morgenthau would quickly conclude that, like American leaders during the "war in Indochina," President Bush Jr. and his neoconservative advisers are once more replacing "experience with superstition," that is, as Halper and Clarke put it, "refus[ing] to correct [their] picture of the world in the light of experience" and using "intelligence for the purpose not of adapting policy to reality, but of reinterpreting reality to fit policy." This is what Halper and Clarke call the neoconservatives' "lack of pragmatism."[29]

The neocons share with the idealists a sense of American exceptionalism and the determination that such American values as democracy, individual rights, and free enterprise are worth spreading about the world. The more the world is made over in the American image, the safer Americans will be. But the neoconservatives turn their noses up at other aspects of idealism, such as the support for international law and institutions, collective security, and, obviously, the suggestion that mankind is not bound to eternal conflict. So, essentially, they isolate out the claim that the world should be made over in the American image, making it synonymous with the drive for security and prosperity and, thus, a justification for policies such as regime change and preemptive war—which, after all, are only manifestations of human nature doing its thing in the international community's state of nature.

The Unnational Nature of National Interest

What all these schools have in common is the belief that, at its most basic, national interest is about maintaining the military and economic security of the nation-state. The debate among idealists, realists, neorealists, and neoconservatives is really about the best strategy and tactics to achieve this basic security. However, there are good reasons to believe that even these most fundamental definitions of security are not, in practice, politically approached as truly national except in a rhetorical way. For instance, Samuel Huntington believes that national interests flow from "national identity," with the result that "we have to know who we are before we can know what our interests are." The confusion as to what American national interests really are reflects "social, intellectual and demographic changes . . . [that] have brought into question the validity and reliance of . . . traditional components of American identity." It is this supposed identity crisis that has allowed "subnational commercial interests and transnational and nonnational ethnic interests . . . [to] dominate foreign policy."[30] Huntington believes that this is a contemporary problem, yet, as we have seen, "subnational" commercial interests have been defining national interests from the very founding of the nation, and ethnic groups have been active in this regard throughout much of the twentieth century.

Peter Trubowitz argues in his *Defining the National Interest* that, in the United States, the effort to define the national interest has historically reflected regional tensions growing out of "the uneven nature of the nation's economic development and integration into the world economy."[31] He examines three periods in American history (the 1890s, the 1930s, and the 1980s) in which the nature of the U.S. national interest and its foreign policies was debated. In each case, he asserts, economic shifts affecting different regions of the country caused political realignments that, in turn, altered how security, particularly economic security, was defined and pursued.

Trubowitz concludes: "The very definition of national interest is a product of politics. For all practical purposes the United States does not have a unique 'national interest.'" He may very well be correct. However, he goes on to reduce the politics that define and redefine national interest to economics: "In its strongest form, the imperatives of American capitalism drive American foreign policy: as the needs of capital change, so eventually does the nation's foreign policy." In other words, for Trubowitz, the specialist interest or lobby factor is but a reflection of "political rivalry and conflict among capitalists."[32] Certainly, Trubowitz's work undermines the notion, so glibly put forth by politicians, pundits, and the media, that national interest is a unitary and unchanging notion. However, economic interest groups are only part of the array of lobbies that have now successfully privatized the U.S. national interest.

While Huntington points to an identity crisis as a source of confusion about national interests and Trubowitz makes the concept dependent on sectional turf wars, others would analyze it out of existence altogether. This process of deconstruction is aptly demonstrated in David Clinton's *The Two Faces of National Interest*. At the beginning of his chapter 2, Clinton tells us that "any defense of the national interest bears a heavy burden of proof" against such charges that the concept is "an ambiguous or even meaningless term," in part because "of uncertainty over the relationship of particular interests and the national interest." He quotes an array of researchers who have come to the conclusion that the term *national interest* is simply "a kind of incantation or nostrum of foreign policy" used by different interests in turn. And, because it is liable to capture by multiple interest groups, eventually the situation develops where "a phrase that is made to signify everything may eventually signify nothing."[33]

Some scholars desiring to qualify this assertion have claimed that the process of defining the national interest is a product of a structure of government that allows society's interests to "make their demands upon the political system, bargain and compete within it, and—assuming that the rules governing political action are fairly drawn and administered—arrive at the common good."[34] We may call this (after Adam Smith) the *invisible hand* theory of how society decides what is good for its collective self. As Clinton notes, under these circumstances, the ability of an interest group to capture the process of policy formulation is exactly the proof necessary to demonstrate that the group represents the common good. Describing this sleight of hand as a "fairly standard pluralist doctrine," Clinton quotes two of its advocates, Thomas Cook and Malcolm Moos, who praise "the normal pursuit of individual interests, ideally held to constitute in their sum the more appropriate long-term interest of the nation."[35] However, critics like James Rosenau point out that such an approach must produce an unstable notion of national interest tied to the subjective desires of whatever group is dominant at the moment.[36] Or, as Hans Morgenthau would put it: "One man's opinion would be as good as the next one's, and power to make one opinion prevail over the others in the contest of the marketplace would be the only applicable criterion."[37] Far from being a standard by which policy can be guided toward and focused on a set of long-term, continuous goals, national interest now becomes, as Clinton puts it, "a scorecard of the success or failure of other, smaller collectivities."[38]

Such analyses come close to reducing the theories of both the realists and the idealists to irrelevancy. The real world of competition for power may be primarily domestic. Foreign policy then becomes the competition of the victorious domestic factions of one country against those of another. And, because competing domestic groups have discovered that it is easier to shape foreign policy if they wrap their efforts in the national flag, the eventual end product will be presented as a policy serving the national interest. In this process, Morgenthau's warning about the "contingent elements of personality, prejudice, and subjective preferences, and the weaknesses of intellect," must be seen not as a corruption but as a normative aspect of the decisionmaking process. Where the privatizing of foreign policy is the rule rather than the exception, the wise observer must constantly ask, *Cui bono?* Who benefits?

Conclusion

This work began by offering a theoretical grounding to the often-observed indifference to foreign affairs and policy of a majority of citizens. While I look at the phenomenon within an American context, the assertion that localism is a natural default position for individuals is a universal one. One can, of course, argue—with some justification—that the degree to which localism prevails is historically contingent. In other words, in places such as Europe where nations are relatively small and borders historically insecure, where wars have been frequent and massively disruptive, and where, in the last half of the twentieth century, there has been economic integration in the form of a common market, a conditioned awareness of affairs beyond the local sphere may be relatively high among a significant percentage of the population. Historically, then, it is disruption that seems to overcome localness. And, in terms of war's contribution to this disruption, it must be judged a very high price to pay for movement away from the default position of localism. It also seems reasonable to suggest that long periods of stability and peace would lower both this awareness level and the percentage of those possessing it. Nonetheless, for those living in more isolated environs, which here must include the United States, things are different. Here, localism is less often challenged.

As we have seen, where localism prevails, it creates its own standing risks. A serious risk derives from the lack of knowledge people have about what lies beyond their locality in terms of both space and time. Under these circumstances, local ways of seeing take on an inbred quality, and assumptions and beliefs acquire a level of sanctification. Thus, where localism prevails, untested assumptions may go unchallenged for so long that they take on the power of custom and tradition. These assumptions may derive from religious teaching, sacred versions of history, or just the familiarity of habitual ways of seeing and acting. This situation may produce a particularly dangerous, yet deemed patriotic, set of beliefs. Such beliefs can define enemies and friends on the basis of in-group and out-group profiling. And they often exist untouched by the sins of one's own people, about which one is never taught. Groupthink becomes the norm.

We have seen how the lack of knowledge of things foreign, as well as of a historical awareness relative to foreign events, makes it difficult to react in an appropriately objective way when foreign affairs do intrude into one's local sphere. This, in turn, forces the majority of citizens in the modern world to rely on assumed experts and government officials, as well as media reports, for an interpretation. The same lack of knowledge then makes it impossible to judge the accuracy and objectivity of the interpretation supplied. Thus, indifference and ignorance cement the average citizen into a culturally and historically structured information environment. This is, of course, a generalization. There are individuals who do not fit this description. However, they are a minority. And, even if those relative few with a more broadly informed and objectively based point of view are vocal in their presentation of that point of view, they usually cannot compete with the media-based interpretation of events.

If mass media–based presentations of things foreign, encompassing the views of pundits and government officials, are consistent and prolonged enough, they can create a thought collective among a great number of citizens (a thought collective may be seen as the manifestation of the groupthink beliefs cited above among a large number of people). This thought collective will embody a conditioned picture in peoples' heads of the subject at hand. The American cold war attitude toward communism and the Soviet Union is a good example of such a thought collective. Presently, there are elements within the political, intellectual, and media elites who are trying to build up a similarly negative thought collective around the concept of Islam and Muslims—a process given a major boost by the events of September 11, 2001. Thought collectives can lead to near-habitual patterns of reactions to events that are interpreted within the information environment as threats—that is, as events that, one has come to believe, can intrude in a negative way on one's local space and time. In such a way was the concept of the domino effect used to make events in a far-off place like Vietnam appear to be a long-distance threat to the way of life of Americans at home.

It is one of the unfortunate aspects of the process here described—localness leading to ignorance, leading to a high susceptibility to media manipulation about things nonlocal, leading to the development of thought collectives, leading to the facilitation of the capture of foreign policy by private interests, often leading to exploitation abroad and war—that it takes disaster (such as the loss of a war) to even temporarily disrupt this cycle. So persistent are the belief patterns characteristic of thought collectives, patterns created by incessant media propaganda operating within the context of localness, that only when the consequences of these beliefs become themselves disruptive of local life do people start questioning them. This then leads to an often-abrupt, if temporary, alteration in both the information environment and government policy.

The natural phenomenon of localism also helps explain, in settled times, the Americans' general disinterest in domestic politics beyond their locality, town, or, at most, state. This is reflected in well-documented low voter turnouts for national elections. This situation has effectively turned the United States from a democracy of individual citizens into a democracy of interest groups, or a *factocracy*, that is, into a democracy of groups of citizens who realize that approaching the government as an organized faction is the only practicable way they can have influence. Though the founding fathers would deplore this situation, it has long defined an important aspect of the structural character of American politics.

While most factions are concerned with domestic topics, some are focused on foreign places and events. Sometimes, this is because of ethnic ties to fellows abroad. In essence, such ties make the foreign ancestral homes of some American ethnic groups extensions of their local environment. In other cases, the special interest is economically based and is interested in a foreign place because it is an important source of raw materials and products or a significant market. Whatever might be the motivation of such groups, they are the ones who are beneficiaries of the natural localism of the average citizen. Mass indifference toward foreign matters simply magnifies the influence of well-organized factions over policy formulation in areas of interest to them. In essence, this leads to the privatization of important aspects of U.S. foreign policy.

As we saw in chapter 2, the history of the American factocracy is a long one. Indeed, it starts soon after the nation's founding. The factions of the late eighteenth and the nineteenth centuries that affected foreign policy were almost exclusively economic in nature. It was the power of such factions and their assumptions about the economic requirements for future prosperity that helped drive westward expansion and, eventually, supported overseas imperial and colonial policies. These factions were not always in agreement, and there was sometimes competition between them. But, at almost every point in the history of the nation, factions advocating an expansive and aggressive posture, characterized as the "large policy" in the late nineteenth century, won out. Then, as laid out in chapter 3, the twentieth century saw the factocracy diversify as noneconomic interests learned how to organize and influence foreign policy formulation. If anything, these groups became more effective lobbies than the nation's economic special interests. Thus, chapters 4 and 5 presented detailed investigations of the activities of lobbies that caused the U.S. government to behave in ways that an objective outside observer might consider to be counter to the nation's overall economic interests.

Minimalist Government as a Spur to Factocracy

There are other factors that result from the theme of localness. For instance, it is a curious, if not wholly illogical, fact that the same factions that push for foreign policies that abet their special economic interests often advocate minimal government activities at home. Let the United States act as a "big government" abroad to smooth the way for coaling stations, to open foreign markets, to assure the cooperation of foreign regimes, etc., but domestically let there be minimal government so as to avoid business regulation and to keep taxes low. In other words, in economic terms, such factions desire to insulate the local environment from outside (i.e., big government) influence.

As we move into the twenty-first century, this corollary of localism has become a dominant theme of ruling conservative elements. For instance, neoconservatives, who want a very big U.S. government role in securing nothing less than world domination, have quite comfortably allied with advocates of domestic minimal government. These latter ideologues of small government, as represented by the followers of both Ronald Reagan and George W. Bush, would have the U.S. government's role in society go little beyond the enforcement of laws and the conducting of national defense—and, of course, the clearing away of obstacles to private enterprise and related interests. Historically, this latter position is an archaic late-eighteenth- and early-nineteenth-century point of view reflecting a narrow interpretation of the work of Adam Smith. Nonetheless, it has never died out as an economic ideology and has now found, along with neoconservative militarism, a commanding place within the administration of George W. Bush.

At times, the ideology of minimalist government and the desire to clear away obstacles targeted by private interests (whether Central and South American socialists or, in the case of Iraq, those who would deny the United States control of the country's oil and the right to assure a government friendly to both Washington and Jerusalem) create, when teamed, bizarre results. A good example of this is the radical outsourcing schemes that have led to the Blackwater mercenary scandal. Blackwater is an American-based business founded in 1997. It supplies a number of military-related services to governments around the world, including training, tactical consulting, and the provision of "security personnel."[1] Because the Bush administration favors the outsourcing of what would normally be seen as government activities, it has contracted with Blackwater (among other, similar firms) for the services of thousands of "security contractors" (mercenaries) to perform guard duty and other activities in Iraq. As a private contractor, Blackwater does not come under U.S. military discipline or rules of engagement. The result has been the kind of unchecked violence that is historically associated with the behavior of mercenaries. To this can be added the fact that, under the administration of George W. Bush, the State Department has quadrupled its outlay for private contractors. It now pays out $4 billion a year to private firms to do what, traditionally, the government has done, for instance, provide protection for American diplomats abroad.[2] Thus, it is not only foreign policy formulation that is now privatized.

Factocracy and National Interest

The operation of the Blackwater Corporation in Iraq is only an extreme example of the fact that, for the United States, national interests are all-too-often defined in terms of the private interests of powerful lobbies. Indeed, this work has argued that it has never been very different in America. As noted above, in practice, national interests have normally manifested themselves in terms of the interests of private groups that win out in the competition for influence over the nation's leaders.

Nonetheless, the concept of national interests is alive and well in the rhetoric of politicians and pundits, the pronouncements of diplomats, and the writings of scholars. The major manifestations of this concept, in terms of various schools of thought, were set forth in chapter 6. Somehow, the nation, made up of competing factions, is transformed by both theoreticians and politicians into a unitary national organism. The collective in all its myriad parts stands as one. Yet, despite all the rhetoric devoted to the concept, it is still the case that, in the context of factocracy, the alleged unitary interests of the organism are hard to pin down. Perhaps there are episodes in the history of American foreign policy that can be claimed to reflect a sense of national interest, but these would not represent the normative pattern in policy formulation.

Despite the special interest nature of U.S. foreign policy formulation, some might claim that, in the nineteenth and twentieth centuries, this approach brought forth considerable success: the economic penetration of Central and South America, the taking of colonies in the Pacific and Caribbean, the abetting of the survival of our principal trading partners through two world wars while at the same time establishing world power status, and, in the postwar era, definitively overcoming capitalism's principal competing economic system, that led by the Soviet Union. In each case, the power of the dominant thought collective, operating within a bounded information environment, caused policies, most of which were, ultimately, designed for the promotion of private groups and the survival of the system of private enterprise, to be accepted by the American people as representative of the community's interests.

One major negative consequence of this seeming success of special interest American foreign policy is that much of the population of the non-Western world now opposes the U.S. government. As a result, Americans might, as time goes on, have to pay an ever-higher price for more than just gasoline. Still, given the place of the capitalist economic system within the American thought collective and, most of the time, a slowly rising standard of living for the American middle class, perhaps one can understand why citizens attentive to these matters may deem U.S. foreign policies economically beneficial. However, things get more problematic when, in the twentieth century, ethnically based interest groups enter the scene, sometimes with sufficient political influence to supersede both economic and security interests.

The history of such powerful and long-lasting ethnically based lobbies as those of Cuban Americans and Zionists makes it hard to reconcile their parochial interests with anything but the self-seeking political interests of those politicians who serve as their allies. As we have seen in chapters 4 and 5, such private interests shaping foreign policy offer little or no economic gains but, rather, have, at times, risked valuable alliances that help sustain economic prosperity. While these lobbies claim to promote the security interests of the United States, equal and, perhaps, better arguments can be made that they undermine security. For example, U.S. foreign policy in the Middle East as it has operated over the last sixty years—much of it to the tune of America's Zionist lobby—has had everything to do with the terrorist attacks of September 11, 2001.

Past, Present, and Future

There is little reason to believe that the near future will differ from the past and the present. The manner in which much of American foreign policy is formulated has now taken on the force of custom and tradition. As alluded to above, it is true that individual policies promoted by special interests can be aborted by catastrophic failure. This was the case with the Vietnam War, which was fought for the sake of an ideology of private enterprise qua freedom that had come to underpin the American thought collective. Yet, even when such particular foreign policies lead to disaster, the general pattern of allowing special interests to capture policy is so ingrained that it continues. Perhaps this is contributed to by the possibility that natural localness encourages short historical memories about happenings that do not have local origins. In any case, the present state of affairs allows the same mistakes to be made over and again. Thus, the military and intelligence analyses that explained why the United States lost in Vietnam were also applicable to the likely consequences of attempting to occupy Iraq. Yet such was the power of special interests—this time ideological and ethnic as well as economic—that negative historical precedents were ignored. And disaster was, once more, the outcome.

Why is it that repeated failure cannot break the pattern, make Americans stand back and then undertake a meaningful national discussion on what should be, collectively, their national interests as well as how policy should be formulated? The answer brings us back to the seminal point about ourselves as a nation made at the beginning of this work—we are a nation of individuals the vast majority of whom continue to live in a condition of localism. As such, we have forfeited the process of foreign policy formulation to competing factions with parochial special interests. And those special interest groups have historically evolved into integral parts of a political process/structure that inherently empowers them. Like some corruption of the story of Shangri-la, nightmares periodically awake us, but then we always fall back into slumber.

Under such circumstances, it should come as no surprise that the general population never demands structural change. For instance, fundamental campaign finance reform—a move that would at least make it more difficult for special interests to influence policy both domestic and foreign—is not on the horizon. Thus, interest group politics will continue to define how we do our political business, and we seem to be stuck with this for the foreseeable future. For those who are disappointed with the consequences of this system, the only present answer is to organize new interest groups to challenge those groups you dislike. For, in the American system of politics, *qui tacet consentire videtur,* "the one who is silent is seen to consent."

Notes

1. The Popular Disregard for Foreign Policy

1. Surprisingly, this relative increase seems not to be as great as one would expect. Even in the post-9/11 world, when "homeland security" should be a primary concern, only 41 percent of American citizens cite it among the most important national problems. See Lindsay and Boot, "Red and Blue Voters."

2. See Granitsas, "Tuning Out the World." For a more optimistic assessment of American attitudes toward foreign affairs, see the Public Opinion and Foreign Policy Studies sponsored by the Chicago Council on Foreign Relations, available on the Web at http://www.thechicagocouncil.org/pos_overview.php.

3. Mueller, "Public Opinion and Foreign Policy," 52.

4. Holsti, *Public Opinion and American Foreign Policy*, xiii.

5. For a discussion of these matters, see ibid., chap. 2.

6. Hastedt, *American Foreign Policy*, 16.

7. U.S. State Department statistics indicate that the number of yearly issuances of passports is rising. Still, in 2007, only 18,382,798 passports were issued, most being renewals. See http://travel.state.gov/passport/services/stats/stats_890.html.

8. Granitsas, "Tuning Out the World."

9. Suggestive evidence for natural localness comes in a recent study tracking cell phone use for six months among 100,000 randomly selected non-Americans. The study reveals that human movement has "a high degree of temporal and spatial regularity, each individual being characterized by a time-independent characteristic travel distance and a significant probability to return to a few frequented locations." As a consequence, daily travel for most people seems to take place within a roughly twenty-mile radius (González, Hidalgo, and Barabási, "Understanding Individual Mobility Patterns," 779).

10. Wittkopf and McCormick, "Domestic Sources of American Foreign Policy," xi.

11. See SIQSS, "The Internet Study."

12. Pinker, *How the Mind Works*, 352.

13. Granitsas, "Tuning Out the World."

14. The ignorance and indifference do not have to be only about political and cultural matters. They can be about the condition of the planet as a whole. See Monbiot, "Civilisation Ends."

15. Lippman, *Public Opinion,* 53, 226.

16. Ibid., 226.

17. Posner, *Law, Pragmatism and Democracy,* 206.

18. Lippman, *Public Opinion,* 227. The way the pundits see their interests can make them the mouthpieces of the government. See Barstow, "Pentagon's Hidden Hand."

19. See Tetlock, "How Accurate Are Your Pet Pundits?" See also Tetlock, *Expert Political Judgment.*

20. See McChesney, *Problem of the Media.*

21. Rather's suit can be found at http://www.nytimes.com/packages/pdf/business/20070920_cbs_complaint.pdf. See also Renner's "Andrew Roth on Front Page Depictions of War," which discusses a study of front-page photographic depictions of the war in Iraq and Afghanistan appearing in the *New York Times* and the *San Francisco Chronicle.*

22. Herman and Chomsky, *Manufacturing Consent,* 2.

23. Terry, *U.S. Foreign Policy,* 15.

24. Cline, "Media/Political Bias."

25. Pitt, "Dan Rather's Magnum Opus."

26. The term *thought collective* was first used by Ludwik Fleck in *Genesis and Development of a Scientific Fact* to describe the socially determined collective approach to scientific research.

27. Willingham, "Critical Thinking," 8, 12.

28. Mueller, "Public Opinion and Foreign Policy," 55. See also Strobel, "The CNN Effect."

29. Berkowitz, "Information Age Intelligence," 207.

30. Surowiecki, *The Wisdom of Crowds,* xiii.

31. Pinker, *How the Mind Works,* 307.

32. Hunt, *Ideology and U.S. Foreign Policy,* 2.

33. Janis, *Victims of Groupthink,* 38.

34. Ravenal, *Never Again,* 51.

35. As one scholar has put it, the common assumption is that "the general public will have little or no influence [in shaping foreign policy] and will play a role primarily as the target of elite manipulation" (Holsti, *Public Opinion and American Foreign Policy,* 127, 160).

36. This is the first of Woodrow Wilson's fourteen points. See Neiberg, ed., *World War I Reader,* 291.

37. Root quoted in Holsti, "Public Opinion and Foreign Policy," 345.

38. Morgenthau quoted in ibid., 345.

39. Janis, *Victims of Groupthink,* 191–92.

40. Hunt, *Ideology and U.S. Foreign Policy,* 4.

41. For instance, it was not until May 2004, after the war had turned sour, that the *New York Times* reversed its supportive coverage of the Bush administration's dubious reasons for invasion. See "From the Editors; the *Times* and Iraq."

42. See Alterman, *When Presidents Lie.*

43. White House, "President Delivers State of the Union Address."

44. The executive editor of the *Washington Post,* Leonard Downie, confessed as much in what David Corn has described as a "front page quasi–mea culpa" published on April 1, 2004. "In hindsight," Corn said, the *Post*'s treatment of the government's WMD claim "looks strikingly one-sided." However, it was not hindsight at all. The paper's Pentagon correspondent, Thomas Ricks, had noted right along that, while "the Administration assertions were on the front page," "things that challenged the administration were on A18 on Sunday or A24 on Monday" (Corn, "Media Lessons"). Nor is the *Post*'s situation atypical. See Massing, "End of the News." For general monitoring of news on policy formulation and other issues, see the Fairness and Accuracy in Reporting (FAIR) Web site: http://www.fair.org/.

45. In "Public Opinion and the War with Iraq"—a report issued by the American Enterprise Institute, a conservative think tank that itself supported the war—Karlyn Bowman claims that support for military action against Saddam Hussein, including invasion, was at the mid-70 percent level during the first six months of 2002.

46. Mackay, *Extraordinary Popular Delusions,* 269–70.

47. Lippman, *Public Opinion,* 65. For just how obstinate and dangerous stereotypes can be, see Shenkman, *Just How Stupid Are We?*

48. Janis, *Victims of Groupthink,* 48–49. On the escalation in Vietnam, see Thomson, "How Could Vietnam Happen?" 241ff.

49. White House, "President Bush Delivers Graduation Speech."

2. Formulating Foreign Policy in a Factocracy

1. López Pintor, Gratschew, and Sullivan, "Voter Turnout Rates from a Comparative Perspective." (The report's data are based on figures given by the Federal Elections Commission.) In the hotly contested 2004 presidential election, 59.6 percent of eligible voters turned out at the polls. Historically, this was a relatively high percentage for Americans. Winning politicians tend not to bother too much about the percentages of eligible voters voting. As Tom Stoppard once put it: "It's not voting that's democracy, it's the counting" (a line spoken by the character Dotty in act 1 of Tom Stoppard's 1972 play *Jumpers*).

2. Caprini and Keeter cited in Mindich, *Tuned Out,* 21.

3. Polsby, "Coalition and Faction," 153–54.

4. "Washington's Farewell Address."

5. "To the People of New York."

6. Madison quoted in Kauffmann, "James Madison," 4–5.

7. Kennan, *Cloud of Danger*, 4.

8. "Washington's Farewell Address."

9. "Diplomacy."

10. Corwin, *The President*, 171.

11. Hastedt, *American Foreign Policy*, 161 (69 percent), 165 (quote).

12. "Diplomacy."

13. The other problem is that the U.S. Supreme Court has ruled that money given to politicians to finance their campaigns is a form of free speech.

14. Mead, *Special Providence*, 26.

15. The maintenance of commercial relations with Europe set the parameters of U.S. foreign policy from the achievement of independence on. See Hartsoe, "Commerce and Diplomacy."

16. See Trubowitz, *Defining the National Interest*.

17. For an example of this dilemma, see Van Atta, "Western Lands."

18. See Bowman, "American Foreign Policy," 19.

19. Ibid., 32.

20. Madison quoted in ibid., 34.

21. Belohlavek, "Economic Interest Groups," 483 (Raguet, Biddle), 480 (Astor, Corcoran and Riggs).

22. "Inaugural Address of James Knox Polk."

23. Stockwell, "The CIA and the Gulf War."

24. Polk, "Special Message."

25. Polk, "Third Annual Message."

26. *Journal of the House of Representatives*, 30th Cong., 30th sess., December 22, 1847, 183–84.

27. Whitman quoted in Weinberg, *Manifest Destiny*, 169.

28. Polk, "Fourth Annual Message."

29. See Feifer, *Breaking Open Japan*, 252.

30. Ibid., 190, 182, 190.

31. Schroeder, *Matthew Calbraith Perry*, 250.

32. Feifer, *Breaking Open Japan*, 188.

33. See Osborne, *Empire Can Wait*, esp. chap. 3.

34. Stevens's wire cited in "President Grover Cleveland's Message."

35. Ibid.

36. For a brief history of Hay and his statement, see "John Milton Hay, 1835–1905."

37. See Raico, "American Foreign Policy."

38. See Williams, *Tragedy of American Diplomacy*.

39. Lodge quoted in Werking, "Henry Cabot Lodge," 238–39. Until well into

the post–World War II era, there was an element of fantasy in this notion that the cure for economic ills lay in tapping a vast Eastern market. As Kemmerer, who lived in Shanghai in the 1920s, has pointed out: "Many persons . . . seem unaware of the meagerness of the China market. China's poverty has always been beyond Western imagination" (review of *China Market*, 197).

40. For a brief survey of these arguments, see Stromberg, "The Spanish-American War," pts. 1 and 2.

41. It was Olney's opinion that "it behooves [the United States] to accept a commanding position . . . among the Powers of the earth." And the way to do this was to satisfy the "present crying need of [its] commercial interests" by acquiring "more markets and larger markets" (Olney quoted in Rothbard, "Wall Street," 4).

42. Success in achieving imperial power status would later, in 1899, underpin the Open Door trading policy (particularly aimed at the China markets) put forth by President McKinley and Secretary of State Hay.

43. Cleveland, "American Interests in the Cuban Revolution," xxvii–lxii.

44. Letter quoted in Pratt, "American Business."

45. See Campbell, "American Business Interests."

46. *Chronicle* quoted in ibid., 168.

47. Quoted in Raico, "American Foreign Policy," 3.

48. Pratt, "American Business," 193.

49. Yellow journalism actually takes its name from *The Yellow Kid*, a full-color comic strip that appeared in both the Hearst and the Pulitzer New York papers.

50. Remington and Hearst wires quoted in Giessel, "Black, White and Yellow."

51. See Trask, *War with Spain in 1898*, 56.

52. See Hilderbrand, *Power and People*. See also Paterson, "U.S. Intervention in Cuba."

53. See Pratt, "Large Policy of 1898," which is dated but still fascinating.

54. Ibid., 242.

55. See Mahan, *Influence of Sea Power*, 70, 83–84. See also LaFeber, "Note on Mahan," 677.

56. Pratt, "Large Policy of 1898," 242.

57. Ibid., 234, 221. By 1897, Teddy Roosevelt was telling others: "I should welcome almost any war, for I think this country needs one" ("Timeline").

58. Rothbard, "Wall Street," 5.

59. "From the Diary of General Máximo Gómez."

60. *World* quoted in Sierra, "War for Cuban Independence."

61. The entire process is described in detail in Foner, *Birth of American Imperialism*, vol. 2.

62. Quoted in Stromberg, "The Spanish-American War," pt. 2.

63. Worcester quoted in "U.S., Philippines, Hawaii, Latin America, in the 1920s."

64. McKinley quoted in Rusling, "Interview with President William McKinley," 22.

65. Wilson quoted in Gray, "Factors Constraining Development," 3.

66. Olney quoted in Rothbard, "Wall Street," 4.

67. Ibid., 6 (on Nelson), 4 (treaty quote).

68. Cockcroft, *Latin America*, 130.

69. Gray, "Factors Constraining Development," 5.

70. See Goodman, "Chiquita's Slipping Appeal."

71. Galeano, *Open Veins*, 225, 283.

72. See Weinberg, *Manifest Destiny*, chap. 10.

73. Grandin, *Empire's Workshop*, 23.

3. The Factocracy Diversifies

1. Wittkopf and McCormick, "Domestic Sources of American Foreign Policy," xvi–xix.

2. Smith, *Foreign Attachments*, 2.

3. See Finan, *Palmer Raids to Patriot Act*.

4. Morgan, *Vietnam Lobby*, 33.

5. Ibid., 7 (Diem descriptions), 8 (Mansfield quote).

6. Some liberal members of the AFV began to abandon the organization over the issue of continued support for Diem. As a result, the AFV became a more conservative group as time went on.

7. Morgan, *Vietnam Lobby*, 36 (AFV leader quote), 41 (Kennedy quote).

8. Ibid., 112.

9. Ibid., 144.

10. See Mallinson, *Cyprus*.

11. Brademas quoted in "New Lobby in Town," 11.

12. Ford, *A Time to Heal*, 138.

13. For the War Powers Act of 1973, see http://www.thecre.com/fedlaw/legal22/warpow.htm.

14. Some critics of the neoconservatives have refused to characterize them as an interest group, seeing them instead simply as like-minded individuals practicing "entrepreneurial democracy" (see Herrington, "Two Recent Books That Attack Neoconservatism"). On the other hand, Halper and Clarke devote the first chapter of their *America Alone* to the proposition that the neoconservatives are a "new political interest group."

15. For the early development of the neoconservative movement, see Ehrman, *Rise of Neoconservatism*.

16. See Norton, *Politics of American Empire*; and Kristol, *Neoconservatism*.

17. For a detailed account of the origins of the neoconservatives, see Ehrman, *Rise of Neoconservatism*.

18. Hobbes, *Leviathan*, 143.

19. Ledeen quote in Polman, "Neoconservatives Push for New World Order." Michael Ledeen is the author of such books as *War against the Terror Masters, Machiavelli on Modern Leadership,* and *Freedom Betrayed.*

20. Manichaeus taught that the world was dominated by two warring principles: light (or good) and darkness (or evil) and that mankind had to choose between them.

21. "War Party."

22. To use Carl Oglesby's terms, the "Yankees" have deserted to the "cowboys" (see Oglesby, *The Yankee and Cowboy War*).

23. The saying is attributed to Irving Kristol, the godfather of neoconservatism.

24. Perle quoted in "War Party."

25. Ehrman, *Rise of Neoconservatism,* 104–9.

26. Loughlin, "Rumsfeld on Looting."

27. Wright, "America's Neoconservatives."

28. Abrams quoted in Lobe, "Military Might and Moral Failure."

29. Ehrman, *Rise of Neoconservatism,* 104–9.

30. Ibid., 190.

31. Ibid., 182–83.

32. Perle quote posted on the Web page of the *Christian Science Monitor:* http://www.csmonitor.com/specials/neocon/neoconQuotes.html.

33. See Zakaria, "The Politics of Rage."

34. See "Recent History of the Neoconservatives."

35. White House, "President Bush Discusses Top Priorities."

36. Quotation taken from the "Statement of Principles" as posted in 1997 on the now-defunct Web site of the Project for the New American Century (PNAC). According to Gary Schmitt, the former executive director of the PNAC, a resident scholar at the American Enterprise Institute (AEI), and the director of the AEI's Advanced Strategic Studies program, the PNAC came to a natural end: "When the project started, it was not intended to go forever. That is why we are shutting it down. We would have had to spend too much time raising money for it and it has already done its job. We felt at the time that there were flaws in American foreign policy, that it was neo-isolationist. We tried to resurrect a Reaganite policy. Our view has been adopted. Even during the Clinton administration we had an effect, with Madeleine Albright [then secretary of state] saying that the United States was 'the indispensable nation'. But our ideas have not necessarily dominated. We did not have anyone sitting on Bush's shoulder. So the work now is to see how they are implemented" (quoted in Reynolds, "End of the Neo-Con Dream").

37. This phrase has entered the foreign policy lexicon. See Etzioni, *Security First.*

38. Of course, it is the competition of economic systems that lies at the heart of cold war ideology.

39. See Zinn, *People's History,* 290–91.

4. Privatizing National Interest—the Cuba Lobby

1. "Jorge Mas Canosa, RIP."
2. Morley and McGillion, *Unfinished Business*, 11.
3. Gonzalez-Pando, *The Cuban Americans*, 158 (Mas Canosa quote), 12.
4. Ibid., 15.
5. Morley and McGillion, *Unfinished Business*, 27.
6. Beschloss and Talbott, *At the Highest Levels*, 57 (Baker quote), 156 (Bush quote).
7. Bush and Scowcroft, *A World Transformed*, 163–65.
8. Gunn, "Will Castro Fall?" 148.
9. Dibble, "Dissident's Call for Dialogue."
10. Staffer quoted in Morley and McGillion, *Unfinished Business*, 32.
11. Ibid., 45.
12. Ibid., 41.
13. Torricelli quoted in Marquis and Anderson, "Bush to Sign Cuba Bill."
14. Morley and McGillion, *Unfinished Business*, 49.
15. Kiger, *Squeeze Play*, 35.
16. Watson quoted in Morley and McGillion, *Unfinished Business*, 57.
17. Ibid., 64 (National Security Council official quote), 56 (Nuccio quote). Nonetheless, by 1995, when the Clinton administration had lost the full confidence of CANF, it would belatedly try to put together a more moderate counterweight to the Cuba lobby (ibid., 90–91).
18. Press Conference of the Secretary of State, May 27, 1993, quoted in ibid., 55.
19. Clinton quoted in Vanderbush and Haney, "Policy toward Cuba," 397. Soon after the president issued this reminder, the Democratic Party received donations from Cuban Americans totaling some $500,000 (see Morley and McGillion, *Unfinished Business*, 65).
20. Gore quoted in Constable, "Clinton Is Urged to Lift Cuban Embargo."
21. Morley and McGillion, *Unfinished Business*, 69 (Skol quote), 55.
22. Between August 21 and August 25, 1994, some twelve thousand rafters were picked up by the U.S. Coast Guard.
23. Nordheimer, "Cuban Group Forges Links."
24. Morley and McGillion, *Unfinished Business*, 75.
25. Ibid., 57.
26. Ibid., 58 (no longer a threat), 159 ("domestic concerns"), 67 ("policy . . . based on economic sanctions").
27. See ibid., 82.
28. Ibid., 90, 103. One immediate consequence of the law was the cessation of all Cuban cooperation on the issue of the interdiction of illegal drugs. This allowed anti-Castro congressmen and senators to repeatedly allege, despite a total

lack of evidence, that Havana was involved in smuggling drugs into the United States (ibid., 107).

29. See ibid., 107.

30. Chrétien quoted in Swardson, "Allies Irked by Bill."

31. Rohter, "Latin American Nations Rebuke U.S."

32. Myers, "Clinton Troubleshooter."

33. Workman quoted in Morley and McGillion, *Unfinished Business,* 114.

34. Ibid., 158.

35. Bush quoted in Smith, "Bush's Dysfunctional Cuba Policy."

36. White House, "Remarks by the President."

37. Quoted in DeYoung, "More US Aid Sought."

38. Quoted in Carter, "Bush Weighs Helms-Burton Law."

39. Powell quoted in Morley and McGillion, *Unfinished Business,* 191.

40. Wilkerson quoted in "Changing Course on Cuba," 3. The same editorial quotes Wayne Smith, the former chief of staff of the U.S. interests section in Havana, as stating: "Cuba seems to have the same effect on American administrations that the full moon has on werewolves."

41. Castro, "Miami Vice," 27.

42. U.S. Department of State, "Remarks by the President on Cuba Policy."

5. Privatizing National Interest—the Israel Lobby

1. Washington quoted in Goldberg, *Jewish Power,* 83.

2. See Curry and Brown, eds., *Conspiracy.*

3. See Birmingham, *Our Crowd.*

4. Goldberg, *Jewish Power,* 98.

5. For the story of the East European Jewish emigration to the United States, see Birmingham, *The Rest of Us.*

6. Goldberg, *Jewish Power,* 102.

7. Coolidge quoted in ibid., 111.

8. See Davidson, *America's Palestine,* 165–68.

9. Goldberg, *Jewish Power,* 119.

10. Ibid., 128.

11. See Urofsky, *American Zionism,* 420 (on ZOA membership in 1941), 407–29 (generally).

12. Ibid., 422.

13. House resolution and Wagner quoted in Davidson, *America's Palestine,* 160 (and see generally chap. 2).

14. Hitti quoted in ibid., 161.

15. *Times* quoted in ibid.

16. Strategists quoted in ibid., 138.

17. *Times* quoted in ibid., 161.

18. Stimson and Hull quoted in ibid., 164, 162.

19. Iraqi communiqué quoted and Marshall cited in ibid., 162.

20. Taft in the *Times* quoted in ibid., 162–63.

21. Roosevelt's statement and Murray quoted in ibid., 163.

22. Both quotes in ibid.

23. Ibid.

24. The most recent example of this phenomenon is the House Foreign Affairs Committee decision to pass a resolution officially endorsing the claim of an Armenian genocide by Turkey during World War I. This has been done even though President Bush has said that such a move "would do great harm to our relations with a key NATO ally" (quoted in Zakaria and Cornwell, "House Panel OKs Armenian Genocide Resolution"). A letter sent to the committee signed by all eight living former secretaries of state also opposed the resolution. House Speaker Nancy Pelosi at first stated that she would bring the resolution to the full House "perhaps by mid-November" (quoted in Thompson, "Ex-Congressmen Lobby Hard"). She began to have second thoughts only when support for the resolution started to slacken, which happened only after Turkey recalled its ambassador from Washington and implicitly threatened to interfere with the 70 percent of all Iraq-bound American air cargo supplies going through Incirlik air base in eastern Turkey. See Torchia, "Turkey Threatens Repercussions"; and Peterson, "Turkish Ire."

25. Goldberg, *Jewish Power,* 136.

26. Ibid., 137.

27. Ibid., 145.

28. See http://www.aipac.org.

29. Smith, *Foreign Agents,* 19.

30. Tivnan, *The Lobby,* 35 (Kenen and Eban, Lipsky quote), 49 (Fulbright hearings).

31. Goldberg, *Jewish Power,* 154. The Foreign Agents Registration Act requires all organizations and individuals who receive money or take direction from foreign governments to register as agents of those governments. AIPAC has always denied that it took either money or direction from Israel. As demonstrated by Smith in *Foreign Agents,* both denials are false.

32. Tivnan, *The Lobby,* 60–61.

33. Ibid., 157.

34. See Davidson, *America's Palestine,* chap. 8.

35. Tivnan, *The Lobby,* 59 (Johnson quote and Johnson's sources).

36. Benin, "Pro-Israel Hawks."

37. Mearsheimer and Walt, *Israel Lobby,* 154. Mearsheimer and Walt might as well have added in the Democratic and Republican parties. The figures vary, but even the conservative sources estimate that at least 40 percent of Democratic funding comes from Jewish American organizations and individuals, and some

have estimated the proportion is as high as 60 percent. The Republican Party receives between 30 and 35 percent of its funding from Jewish sources. As a consequence, when AIPAC held its 2002 annual conference, half the Senate and a third of the House made what was almost an obligatory appearance.

38. This was the doing of Thomas Dine. According to Christison and Christison's "The Power of the Israel Lobby": "Dine believed that anyone who could provide policymakers with books and papers focusing on Israel's strategic value to the U.S. would effectively 'own' the policymakers."

39. Goldberg, *Jewish Power,* 167.

40. Anti-Communist organized labor lobbyists working through the Illinois senator Adlai Stevenson III tied an amendment onto routine legislation that cut import tax credits to the Soviets and, thus, made most-favored-nation status useless to them. This was another example of lobbyists placing their parochial interests above the national interest.

41. Goldberg, *Jewish Power,* 178.

42. Ibid., 198.

43. Begin was considered a terrorist ringleader by the British during the later Mandate period.

44. Goldberg, *Jewish Power,* 220.

45. This connection was recently attested to by Akiva Eldar, the chief political columnist of Israel's *Haaretz* newspaper. In a series of talks given in the United States on October 1 and 2, 2007, Eldar asserted that the Israel lobby in the United States takes its direction from the right wing of the Israeli power structure. See HaLevi, "Haaretz Editor Says 'the Settlers' Control Israel Lobby." See also Curtiss, *Stealth PACs;* Findley, *Deliberate Deceptions;* and Findley, ed., *They Dare Not Speak Out.*

46. In 2005, the Department of Justice indicted two AIPAC staff members, Steven Rosen and Keith Weissman, on charges of espionage, claiming that they had passed secret government information, obtained illegally from a disgruntled Pentagon analyst, to an Israeli diplomat. The opening of this trial, originally scheduled for early 2008, has been repeatedly delayed. Part of the reason is that the presiding judge has insisted on an unusually high burden of proof for conviction. For instance, the prosecution must prove that the defendants not only violated the law by passing secrets to Israel but also "had a bad-faith reason to believe the disclosures could be used to the injury of the United States or to the aid of a foreign nation" (quoted in Guttman, "Appeals Court Sets High Bar").

47. Goldberg, *Jewish Power,* 208.

48. Rabbi Arthur Lelyveld, President of the Reform Rabbinate, quoted in ibid., 207.

49. Ibid., 208.

50. Ibid., 211.

51. Ibid., 213.

52. Christison and Christison, "The Power of the Israel Lobby." It is interesting to note that, early in President Carter's term of office, Menachem Begin had tried to promote the idea of Israel as a "strategic Cold War asset" to the United States. However, Carter came to the conclusion, not only that Israel was not such an asset, but also that its behavior toward Egypt and the Palestinians made it a liability (ibid.). Carter's attempt to bring about an Arab-Israeli peace at Camp David can be seen, in part, as an effort to change Israel's liability status. On the other hand, Reagan essentially surrendered U.S. Middle East policy formulation to the Zionists.

53. Goldberg, *Jewish Power,* 214.

54. Tivnan, *The Lobby,* 11.

55. Goldberg, *Jewish Power,* 217, 218.

56. Lautenberg quoted in ibid., 265. Things have not changed much since 1987. In September 2004, e.g., the *Washington Post* reported Representative Dave Obey, the ranking Democrat on the House Appropriations Committee, as stating that AIPAC has "pushed the Likud Party line and in the process has crowded out other voices in the Jewish community, especially those pressing for withdrawal from West Bank settlements as a concession in the peace process" (Edsall and Moore, "Pro-Israel Lobby Has Strong Voice").

57. Benin, "Pro-Israel Hawks."

58. While he was Israel's ambassador to the United States, Yitzhak Rabin liked to assert that the Israel lobby was never under his control. However, in his memoirs, he makes it plain that the Israeli government thought of the lobby as an adjunct to Israeli policy to be used as Jerusalem "saw fit" (Rabin, *The Rabin Memoirs,* 229). As Edward Tivan has pointed out, Rabin cannot have it both ways. The reality of the situation was that the "very status of the leadership of the American Jewish community rested on Israel's good will" (Tivnan, *The Lobby,* 77).

59. Smith, "The AIPAC Story."

60. Goldberg, *Jewish Power,* 224.

61. Only rarely has Congress formally investigated this foreign agent issue as it relates to the Israel lobby. The most revealing investigation was in 1963, during the hearings held by Senator William Fulbright and the Senate Foreign Relations Committee. The inquiry led to no important change in American Zionist behavior in relation to the U.S. government.

62. Mearsheimer and Walt, *Israel Lobby,* 231ff. See also Christison and Christison, "The Teflon Alliance with Israel," and "Too Many Smoking Guns to Ignore."

63. Mearsheimer and Walt, *Israel Lobby,* 229–62.

64. Chomsky, "The Israel Lobby."

65. Massad, "Blaming the Lobby."

66. Rubenberg, *Israel and the American National Interest,* 7.

6. Is There a National Interest?

1. *Power* here means not only physical force but also the ability to influence, manipulate, and command.

2. Morgenthau, *Politics among Nations,* 5 (quote), 6–8.

3. Clinton, *Two Faces of National Interest,* 31.

4. Ibid., 6.

5. Morgenthau, *Politics among Nations,* 4–15.

6. Ibid. See also Morgenthau, "Deluding Ourselves in Vietnam."

7. Morgenthau, *Politics among Nations,* principle 4.

8. Kennan, *American Diplomacy,* 95, 96.

9. "Through the Realist Lens: Conversation with John Mearsheimer."

10. Morgenthau, *Politics among Nations,* 8–9, principle 5.

11. Hunt, *Ideology and U.S. Foreign Policy,* 7.

12. Waltz, *Theory of International Relations,* 188.

13. See Brooks, "Dueling Realisms," 12.

14. See "Beliefs about Foreign Policy."

15. See Davidson, *America's Palestine,* 15–21.

16. See ibid.

17. "American Idealism and Foreign Policy."

18. See Jacoby, "Did Carter Fail on Human Rights?"

19. Yglesias, "Neoconservative Idealism."

20. Bush quoted in Jacoby, "Did Carter Fail on Human Rights?"

21. Yglesias, "Neoconservative Idealism."

22. Krauthammer, "Neoconservatism and Foreign Policy."

23. Halper and Clarke, *America Alone,* 9, 10.

24. Kristol, "Neoconservative Persuasion."

25. Ibid., 11.

26. Ibid., 12, 19.

27. Krauthammer, "Neoconservatism and Foreign Policy."

28. See McAlister, *Epic Encounters,* chap. 4.

29. Halper and Clarke, *America Alone,* 21.

30. Huntington, "Erosion of American National Interests," 12.

31. Trubowitz, *Defining the National Interest,* 4.

32. Ibid., 12, 10.

33. Clinton, *Two Faces of National Interest,* 21–22.

34. Trubowitz, *Defining the National Interest,* 26. On this approach to the common good, see Bentley, *The Process of Government,* 222. See also Beard, *The Idea of National Interest,* 167.

35. Clinton, *Two Faces of National Interest,* 26 (quoting Cook and Moos, "American Idea of International Interest").

36. Rosenau, "National Interest."

37. Morgenthau quoted in Clinton, *Two Faces of National Interest,* 32.
38. Ibid., 27.

Conclusion

1. See the Blackwater USA Web site: www.blackwaterusa.com.
2. See Broder and Rohde, "Use of Contractors by State Department."

Bibliography

Abboud, Edward. *Invisible Enemy: Israel, Politics, Media and American Culture.* Reston, VA: Vox, 2003.

Alterman, Eric. *What Liberal Media? The Truth about Bias and the News.* New York: Basic, 2003.

———. *When Presidents Lie.* New York: Viking, 2004.

"American Idealism and Foreign Policy." Pt. 5 of "U.S. Foreign Policy and the Bush Administration: Conversation with James Fallows." Conversations with History, Institute of International Studies, University of California, Berkeley, March 28, 2005. http://globetrotter.berkeley.edu/people5/Fallows/fallows-con5.html.

Barstow, David. "Behind TV Analysts, the Pentagon's Hidden Hand." *New York Times,* April 20, 2008, 1, 24–26.

Beard, Charles. *The Idea of National Interest: An Analytical Study in American Foreign Policy.* New York: Macmillan, 1934.

"Beliefs about Foreign Policy." Pt. 4 of "Foreign Policy Attitudes Now Driven by 9/11 and Iraq." Pew Research Center, Survey Report, August 18, 2004. http://people-press.org/reports/display.php3?PageID=866.

Belohlavek, John M. "Economic Interest Groups and the Formation of Foreign Policy in the Early Republic." *Journal of the Early Republic* 14, no. 4 (Winter 1994): 476–84.

Benin, Joel. "Pro-Israel Hawks and the Second Gulf War." *Middle East Report Online,* April 6, 2003. http://www.merip.org/mero/mero040603.html.

Bentley, Arthur F. *The Process of Government: A Study of Social Pressures.* 1908. Edited by Peter H. Odegard. Cambridge, MA: Harvard University Press, 1967.

Berkowitz, Bruce D. "Information Age Intelligence." In *The Domestic Sources of American Foreign Policy: Insights and Evidence* (3rd ed.), ed. Eugene R. Wittkopf and James M. McCormick. Lanham, MD: Rowman & Littlefield, 1999.

Beschloss, M., and S. Talbott. *At the Highest Levels.* London: Warner, 1993.

Birmingham, Stephen. *Our Crowd: The Great Jewish Families of New York.* New York: Tess, 1967.

————. *The Rest of Us: The Rise of America's Eastern European Jews*. Boston: Little, Brown, 1984.

Bowman, Albert. "Jefferson, Hamilton and American Foreign Policy." *Political Science Quarterly* 71, no. 1 (March 1956): 18–41.

Bowman, Karlyn. "Public Opinion and the War with Iraq." Washington, DC: American Enterprise Institute, 2008. http://www.aei.org/publications/pubID.22142/pub_detail.asp.

Broder, John M., and David Rohde. "Use of Contractors by State Department Has Soared." *New York Times,* October 24, 2007.

Brooks, Stephen G. "Dueling Realisms (Realism in International Relations)." *International Organization* 51, no. 3 (Summer 1997): 445–77.

Bush, George, and Brent Scowcroft. *A World Transformed.* New York: Knopf, 1998.

Campbell, Charles, Jr. "American Business Interests and the Open Door in China." *Far Eastern Quarterly* 1, no. 1 (November 1941): 44–52.

Carter, Tom. "Bush Weighs Helms-Burton Law." *Washington Times,* June 11, 2001.

Castro, Max J. "Miami Vice." *The Nation,* May 14, 2007, 26–32.

"Changing Course on Cuba." *The Nation,* May 14, 2007, 3.

Chomsky, Noam. "The Israel Lobby." ZNet, March 28, 2006. http://www.zmag.org/znet/viewArticle/4134.

Christison, Kathleen, and Bill Christison. "Too Many Smoking Guns to Ignore." *Counterpunch,* January 25, 2003. http://www.counterpunch.org/christison01252003.html.

————. "The Power of the Israel Lobby." *Counterpunch,* June 16/18, 2006. http://www.counterpunch.org/christison06162006.html.

————. "The Teflon Alliance with Israel." *Counterpunch,* September 28, 2007. http://www.counterpunch.org/christison09272007.html.

Cleveland, Grover. "American Interests in the Cuban Revolution." In *Papers Relating to Foreign Policy, 1896.* Washington, DC: U.S. Department of State, 1897.

Cline, Andrew R. "Media/Political Bias." *Rhetorica,* Spring 2002. http://rhetorica.net/bias.htm.

Clinton, W. David. *The Two Faces of National Interest.* Baton Rouge: Louisiana State University Press, 1994.

Cockcroft, James D. *Latin America: History, Politics and U.S. Policy.* 2nd ed. Chicago: Nelson-Hall, 1996.

Constable, P. "Clinton Is Urged to Lift Cuban Embargo but Firm Policy Still in Place." *Boston Globe,* May 13, 1993.

Cook, Thomas, and Malcolm Moos. "The American Idea of International Interest." *American Political Science Review* 47 (March 1953): 31–42.

Corn, David. "Media Lessons." TomPaine.common sense, August 18, 2004. http://www.tompaine.com/articles/media_lessons.php.

Corwin, Edward S. *The President: Office and Powers, 1787–1957.* New York: New York University Press, 1957.

Curry, Richard O., and Thomas M. Brown, eds. *Conspiracy: The Fear of Subversion in American History.* New York: Holt, Rinehart & Winston, 1972.

Curtiss, Richard H. *Stealth PACs: How Israel's American Lobby Took Control of U.S. Middle East Policy.* Washington, DC: American Educational Trust, 1990.

Davidson, Lawrence. *America's Palestine: Popular and Official Perceptions from Balfour to Israeli Statehood.* Gainesville: University Press of Florida, 2001.

DeYoung, Karen. "More US Aid Sought for Cuban Dissidents." *Washington Post,* March 8, 2001.

Dibble, Sandra. "Dissident's Call for Dialogue Ignites Exiles." *Miami Herald,* June 22, 1990.

"Diplomacy: The State Department at Work." Washington, DC: U.S. Department of State, Bureau of Public Affairs, July 2001. http://www.state.gov/r/pa/ei/rls/dos/4078.htm.

Edsall, Thomas B., and Molly Moore. "Pro-Israel Lobby Has Strong Voice: AIPAC Is Embroiled in Investigation of Pentagon Leaks." *Washington Post,* September 5, 2004. http://www.washingtonpost.com/wp-dyn/articles/A62438-2004Sep4.html.

Ehrman, John. *The Rise of Neoconservatism: Intellectuals and Foreign Affairs, 1945–1994.* New Haven, CT: Yale University Press, 1995.

Etzioni, Amitai. *Security First: For a Muscular, Moral Foreign Policy.* New Haven, CT: Yale University Press, 2007.

Feifer, George. *Breaking Open Japan.* New York: HarperCollins, 2006.

Finan, Charles M. *From the Palmer Raids to the Patriot Act.* Boston: Beacon, 2007.

Findley, Paul, ed. *They Dare Not Speak Out: People and Institutions Confront Israel's Lobby.* Chicago: Lawrence Hill, 1989.

———. *Deliberate Deceptions: Facing the Facts about the U.S.-Israeli Relationship.* Washington, DC: American Educational Trust, 1995.

Fleck, Ludwik. *The Genesis and Development of a Scientific Fact.* Chicago: University of Chicago Press, 1979.

Foner, Philip. *The Spanish-Cuban-American War and the Birth of American Imperialism.* 2 vols. New York: Monthly Review Press, 1972.

Ford, Gerald. *A Time to Heal: The Autobiography of Gerald Ford.* New York: Harper & Row, 1979.

"From the Diary of General Máximo Gómez." January 8, 1899. Excerpted at http://www.historyofcuba.com/history/gomez.htm.

"From the Editors; the *Times* and Iraq." *New York Times,* May 26, 2004. Available at http://www.nytimes.com/.

Galeano, Eduardo. *Open Veins of Latin America.* New York: Monthly Review Press, 1973.

Giessel, Jess. "Black, White and Yellow: Journalism and Correspondents of the Spanish-American War." Spanish-American War Centennial Website, 2005. http://www.spanamwar.com/press.htm.

Goldberg, J. J. *Jewish Power: Inside the American Jewish Establishment.* Reading, MA: Addison-Wesley, 1996.

González, Marta C., César A. Hidalgo, and Albert-László Barabási. "Understanding Individual Human Mobility Patterns." *Nature* 453, no. 7196 (June 5, 2008): 779–82.

Gonzalez-Pando, Miguel. *The Cuban Americans.* Westport, CT: Greenwood, 1998.

Goodman, Amy. "Chiquita's Slipping Appeal." AlterNet, March 21, 2007. http://www.alternet.org/columnists/story/49588/.

Grandin, Greg. *Empire's Workshop: Latin America, the United States, and the Rise of the New Imperialism.* New York: Henry Holt, 2006.

Granitsas, Alkman. "Americans Are Tuning Out the World." *YaleGlobal Online,* November 24, 2005. http://yaleglobal.yale.edu/article.print?id=6553.

Gray, Alexander. "Factors Constraining Development in Central America." *History Studies* (University of Limerick), November 2000.

Gunn, Gillian. "Will Castro Fall?" *Foreign Policy,* no. 79 (Summer 1989): 132–50.

Guttman, Nathan. "In Espionage Trial of Ex-Aipac Employees, Appeals Court Sets High Bar for Prosecution." *Jewish Daily Forward,* June 20, 2008. http://www.forward.com/articles/13629/.

HaLevi, Ezra. "Haaretz Editor Says 'the Settlers' Control Israel Lobby." *Israel National News,* October 7, 2007. http://www.israelnationalnews.com/News/News.aspx/123842.

Halper, Stefan, and Jonathan Clarke. *America Alone: The Neo-Conservatives and the Global Order.* New York: Cambridge University Press, 2004.

Hartsoe, Kenneth D. "Commerce and Diplomacy: The First Year of American Foreign Policy, 1775–1776." *Early America Review,* Summer/Fall 2002. http://www.earlyamerica.com/review/2002_summer_fall/foreign_policy.htm.

Hastedt, Glenn P. *American Foreign Policy: Past, Present, Future.* 5th ed. Upper Saddle River, NJ: Prentice-Hall, 2003.

Herman, Edward S., and Noam Chomsky. *Manufacturing Consent: The Political Economy of the Mass Media.* New York: Pantheon, 1988.

Herrington, Matt. "Two Recent Books That Attack Neoconservatism: Are They Persuasive?" FindLaw: Legal News and Commentary, April 22, 2005. http://writ.news.findlaw.com/books/reviews/20050422_herrington.html.

Hersman, Rebecca K. C. *Friends and Foes: How Congress and President Really Make Foreign Policy.* Washington, DC: Brookings, 2000.

Hilderbrand, Robert C. *Power and People: Executive Management of Public Opin-*

ion in Foreign Policy, 1897–1921. Chapel Hill: University of North Carolina Press, 1981.

Hobbes, Thomas. *Leviathan.* 1651. Cleveland: Meridian, 1963.

Holsti, Ole R. "Public Opinion and Foreign Policy: Challenges to the Almond-Lippmann Consensus." In *American Foreign Policy: Theoretical Essays* (4th ed.), ed. G. John Ikenberry. New York: Addison-Wesley, 2002.

———. *Public Opinion and American Foreign Policy.* Rev. ed. Ann Arbor: University of Michigan Press, 2004.

Hunt, Michael H. *Ideology and U.S. Foreign Policy.* New Haven, CT: Yale University Press, 1987.

Huntington, Samuel P. "The Erosion of American National Interests." In *The Domestic Sources of American Foreign Policy: Insights and Evidence* (3rd ed.), ed. Eugene R. Wittkopf and James M. McCormick. Lanham, MD: Rowman & Littlefield, 1999.

Ikenberry, G. John, ed. *American Foreign Policy: Theoretical Essays.* 4th ed. New York: Addison-Wesley, 2002.

"Inaugural Address of James Knox Polk." March 4, 1845. http://www.yale.edu/lawweb/avalon/presiden/inaug/polk.htm.

Jacoby, Tamar. "Did Carter Fail on Human Rights?" *Washington Monthly,* December 6, 1986.

Janis, Irving L. *Victims of Groupthink.* Atlanta: Houghton Mifflin, 1972.

"John Milton Hay, 1835–1905." n.d. In "The World of 1898: The Spanish-American War." Hispanic Reading Room, Library of Congress. http://www.loc.gov//rr/hispanic/1898/hay.html.

"Jorge Mas Canosa, RIP." *National Review,* December 31, 1997, 63.

Kagan, Robert, and William Kristol, eds. *Present Dangers: Crisis and Opportunity in American Foreign and Defense Policy.* San Francisco: Encounter, 2000.

Kamalipour, Yahya R. *The U.S. Media and the Middle East: Image and Perception.* Westport, CT: Praeger, 1995.

Kauffmann, Bruce G. "James Madison, 'Godfather of the Constitution.'" *Early America Review,* Summer 1997. http://www.earlyamerica.com/review/summer97/madison.html.

Kemmerer, Donald L. Review of Thomas McCormick, *China Market: America's Quest for Informal Empire, 1893–1901. Annals of the American Academy of Political and Social Science* 377 (May 1968): 197.

Kennan, George F. *American Diplomacy, 1900–1950.* Chicago: University of Chicago Press, 1951.

———. *The Cloud of Danger: Current Realities of American Foreign Policy.* New York: Little, Brown, 1977.

Kiger, Patrick J. *Squeeze Play: The United States, Cuba and the Helms-Burton Act.* Washington, DC: Center for Public Integrity, 1997.

Krauthammer, Charles. "Neoconservatism and Foreign Policy." *In the National*

Interest, Fall 2004. http://www.inthenationalinterest.com/Articles/October 2004/October2004Krauthammer.html.

Kristol, Irving. *Neoconservatism: The Biography of an Idea.* New York: Free Press, 1995.

———. "The Neoconservative Persuasion." *Weekly Standard,* August 25, 2003. http://www.weeklystandard.com/Content/Public/Articles/000/000/003/000tzmlw.asp.

Kull, Steven, and I. M. Destler. *Misreading the Public: The Myth of a New Isolationism.* Washington, DC: Brookings, 1999.

LaFeber, Walter. "A Note on the Mercantilistic Imperialism of Alfred Thayer Mahan." *Mississippi Valley Historical Review* 48, no. 4 (March 1962): 519–22.

Larson, Eric V. *Casualties and Consensus: The Historical Role of Casualties in Domestic Support for U.S. Military Operations.* Santa Monica, CA: Rand, 1996.

Ledeen, Michael A. *Freedom Betrayed: How America Led a Global Democratic Revolution, Won the Cold War, and Walked Away.* Washington, DC: American Enterprise Institute Press, 1996.

———. *Machiavelli on Modern Leadership: Why Machiavelli's Iron Rules Are as Timely and Important Today as Five Centuries Ago.* New York: Truman Talley, 1999.

———. *The War against the Terror Masters: Why It Happened, Where We Are Now, How We'll Win.* New York: St. Martin's, 2002.

Lindsay, James M., and Max Boot. "On Foreign Policy, Red and Blue Voters Are Worlds Apart: Commentary on the National Council/Pew Poll." Council on Foreign Relations, August 18, 2004. http://www.cfr.org/publication/7259.

Lippman, Walter. *Public Opinion.* New York: Free Press, 1997.

Lobe, Jim. "Military Might and Moral Failure." *Asia Times,* August 13, 2003.

López Pintor, Rafael, Maria Gratschew, and Kate Sullivan. "Voter Turnout Rates from a Comparative Perspective." In *Voter Turnout since 1945: A Global Report.* Stockholm: International Idea, 2002. http://www.idea.int/publications/vt/upload/voter%20turnout.pdf.

Loughlin, Sean. "Rumsfeld on Looting in Iraq: 'Stuff Happens.'" CNN.com, April 12, 2003. http://www.cnn.com/2003/US/04/11/sprj.irq.pentagon/.

Mackay, Charles. *Extraordinary Popular Delusions and the Madness of Crowds.* New York: Three Rivers, 1980.

Mahan, Alfred Thayer. *The Influence of Sea Power upon History.* Boston: Little, Brown, 1898.

Mallinson, William. *Cyprus: A Modern History.* London: I. B. Tauris, 2005.

Marquis, C., and P. Anderson. "Bush to Sign Cuba Bill in Miami." *Miami Herald,* October 23, 1992.

Massad, Joseph. "Blaming the Lobby." *Al-Ahram Weekly,* March 23–29, 2006. http://weekly.ahram.org.eg/2006/787/op35.htm.

Massing, Michael. "The End of the News." *New York Review of Books* 52, no. 19 (December 1, 2005): 23–27.

McAlister, Melani. *Epic Encounters: Culture, Media and U.S. Interests in the Middle East, 1945–2000.* Berkeley and Los Angeles: University of California Press, 2001.

McChesney, Robert W. *The Problem of the Media: U.S. Communication Politics in the 21st Century.* New York: Monthly Review Foundation, 2004.

Mead, Walter Russell. *Special Providence: American Foreign Policy and How It Changed the World.* New York: Routledge, 2002.

Mearsheimer, John J., and Stephen M. Walt. *The Israel Lobby and U.S. Foreign Policy.* New York: Farrar Straus Giroux, 2007.

Mindich, David T. Z. *Tuned Out: Why Americans under 40 Don't Follow the News.* New York: Oxford University Press, 2005.

Monbiot, George. "Civilisation Ends with a Shutdown of Human Concern: Are We There Already?" *Guardian,* October 30, 2007. http://www.guardian.co.uk/commentisfree/2007/oct/30/comment.books.

Morgan, Joseph. *The Vietnam Lobby: The American Friends of Vietnam, 1955–1975.* Chapel Hill, NC: University of North Carolina Press, 1997.

Morgenthau, Hans J. "We Are Deluding Ourselves in Vietnam." *New York Times Magazine,* April 18, 1965.

———. *Politics among Nations: The Struggle for Power and Peace.* 5th ed., rev. New York: Knopf, 1978.

Morley, Morris, and Chris McGillion. *Unfinished Business: America and Cuba after the Cold War, 1989–2001.* New York: Cambridge University Press, 2002.

Mueller, John. *Policy and Opinion in the Gulf War.* Chicago: University of Chicago Press, 1994.

———. "Public Opinion and Foreign Policy: The People's Common Sense." In *The Domestic Sources of American Foreign Policy: Insights and Evidence* (3rd ed.), ed. Eugene R. Wittkopf and James M. McCormick. Lanham, MD: Rowman & Littlefield, 1999.

Myers, Steve Lee. "Clinton Troubleshooter Discovers Big Trouble from Allies on Cuba." *New York Times,* October 23, 1996.

Neiberg, Michael S., ed. *The World War I Reader.* New York: New York University Press, 2006.

"New Lobby in Town: The Greeks." *Time,* July 14, 1975, 11–13.

Nordheimer, Jon. "Cuban Group Forges Links to Clinton." *New York Times,* August 26, 1994.

Norton, Anne. *Leo Strauss and the Politics of American Empire.* New Haven, CT: Yale University Press, 2004.

Oglesby, Carl. *The Yankee and Cowboy War: Conspiracies from Dallas to Watergate.* New York: Berkeley, 1977.

Osborne, Thomas J. *Empire Can Wait: American Opposition to Hawaiian Annexation, 1893–1898.* Kent, OH: Kent State University Press, 1981.

Page, Benjamin I., and Robert Y. Shapiro. *The Rational Public: Fifty Years of Trends in Americans' Policy Preferences.* Chicago: University of Chicago Press, 1992.

Palast, Greg. *The Best Democracy Money Can Buy.* New York: Penguin, 2003.

Paterson, Thomas G. "U.S. Intervention in Cuba, 1898: Interpretations." *History Teacher* 29, no. 3 (May 1996): 5–9.

Peterson, Scott. "Turkish Ire May Affect Iraq War." *Christian Science Monitor,* October 12, 2007.

Petras, James. *The Power of Israel in the United States.* Atlanta: Fernwood, 2006.

Pinker, Steven. *How the Mind Works.* New York: Norton, 1997.

Pitt, William Rivers. "Dan Rather's Magnum Opus." *Truthout,* September 26, 2007. http://www.truthout.org/article/william-rivers-pitt-dan-rathers-magnum-opus.

Polk, James K. "Special Message." May 11, 1846. http://www.presidency.ucsb.edu/ws/index.php?pid=67907.

———. "Third Annual Message." December 7, 1848. http://www.presidency.ucsb.edu/ws/index.php?pid=29488.

———. "Fourth Annual Message." December 5, 1848. http://www.presidency.ucsb.edu/ws/index.php?pid=29489.

Polman, Dick. "Neoconservatives Push for New World Order." *San Jose Mercury News,* May 4, 2003.

Polsby, Nelson. "Coalition and Faction in American Politics: An Institutional View." In *Emerging Coalitions in American Politics,* ed. Seymour Lipset. Piscataway, NJ: Transaction, 1978.

Posner, Richard. *Law, Pragmatism and Democracy.* Cambridge, MA: Harvard University Press, 2003.

Pratt, Julius W. "The Large Policy of 1898." *Mississippi Valley Historical Review* 19, no. 2 (September 1932): 219–42.

———. "American Business and the Spanish-American War." *Hispanic American Historical Review* 14, no. 2 (May 1934): 163–201.

"President Grover Cleveland's Message." December 18, 1893. http://www.hawaii-nation.org/cleveland.html.

Rabin, Yitzhak. *The Rabin Memoirs.* Boston: Little, Brown, 1797.

Raico, Ralph. "American Foreign Policy: The Turning Point, 1898–1919." 6 pts. *Freedom Daily* (Future of Freedom Foundation), February–July 1995. http://www.fff.org/freedom/0295c.asp.

Ravenal, Earl. *Never Again: Learning from America's Foreign Policy Failures.* Philadelphia: Temple University Press, 1978.

"Recent History of the Neoconservatives." Pt. 5 of "The Neoconservatives: Conversation with Jonathan Clarke." Conversations with History, Institute of International Studies, University of California, Berkeley, April 4, 2005. http://globetrotter.berkeley.edu/people5/Clarke/clarke-con5.html.

Renner, Matt. "Andrew Roth on Front Page Depictions of War." *Truthout*, January 11, 2008. http://www.truthout.org/article/andrew-roth-front-page-depictions-war.

Reynolds, Paul. "End of the Neo-Con Dream." BBC Online, December 21, 2006. http://news.bbc.co.uk/2/hi/middle_east/6189793.stm.

Rohter, Larry. "Latin American Nations Rebuke U.S. for the Embargo on Cuba." *New York Times*, June 6, 1996.

Rosenau, James. "National Interest." In vol. 11 of *International Encyclopedia of the Social Sciences*, ed. David Sills. New York: Macmillan, 2007.

Rothbard, Murry N. "Wall Street, Banks, and American Foreign Policy." *World Market Perspective*, August 1984, 4. Available at http://www.lewrockwell.com/rothbard/rothbard66.html.

Rubenberg, Cheryl. *Israel and the American National Interest*. Urbana: University of Illinois Press, 1986.

Rusling, James. "Interview with President William McKinley." *The Christian Advocate*, January 22, 1903. Reprinted in *The Philippines Reader*, ed. Daniel B. Schirmer and Stephen Rosskamm Shalom. Boston: South End Press, 1987.

Schroeder, John H. *Matthew Calbraith Perry: Antebellum Sailor and Diplomat*. Annapolis, MD: Naval Institute Press, 2001.

Serfaty, Simon, ed. *The Media and Foreign Policy*. New York: St. Martin's, 1991.

Shenkman, Richard. *Just How Stupid Are We? Facing the Truth about the American Voter*. New York: Basic, 2008.

Sierra, Jerry A. "The War for Cuban Independence: Pt. 4, After the War." First posted in 1996. http://www.historyofcuba.com/history/scaw/scaw3.htm.

Smith, Grant F. *Foreign Agents*. Washington, DC: Institute for Research, Middle East Policy, 2007.

Smith, Sam. "The AIPAC Story." *Progressive Review*, March 2003. Available at http://www.thirdworldtraveler.com/Israel/AIPAC_Story.html.

Smith, Tony. *Foreign Attachments: The Power of Ethnic Groups in the Making of American Foreign Policy*. Cambridge, MA: Harvard University Press, 2002.

Smith, Wayne S. "Bush's Dysfunctional Cuba Policy." *Foreign Policy in Focus*, November 6, 2006. http://www.fpif.org/fpiftxt/3675.

Sobel, Richard. *The Impact of Public Opinion on U.S. Foreign Policy since Vietnam*. New York: Oxford University Press, 2001.

"The Spanish-American War." Small Planet Communications, 2000. http://www.smplanet.com/imperialism/gift.html.

Stanford Institute for the Quantitative Study of Society (SIQSS). "The Internet Study: More Detail." News release, February 16, 2000. http://www.stanford.edu/group/siqss/Press_Release/press_detail.html.

Stockwell, John. "The CIA and the Gulf War." Speech delivered at the Louden Nelson Community Center, Santa Cruz, CA, February 20, 1991.

Strobel, Warren. "The CNN Effect: Myth or Reality?" In *The Domestic Sources of American Foreign Policy: Insights and Evidence* (3rd ed.), ed. Eugene R. Wittkopf and James M. McCormick. Lanham, MD: Rowman & Littlefield, 1999.

Stromberg, Joseph R. "The Spanish-American War: The Leap into Overseas Empire." Pt. 1. *Freedom Daily* (Future of Freedom Foundation), December 1998. http://www.fff.org/freedom/1298e.asp.

———. "The Spanish-American War: The Leap into Overseas Empire." Pt. 2. *Freedom Daily* (Future of Freedom Foundation), January 1999. http://www.fff.org/freedom/0199f.asp.

Surowiecki, James. *The Wisdom of Crowds*. New York: Anchor, 2005.

Swardson, Anne. "Allies Irked by Bill to Deter Their Trade with U.S. Foes." *Washington Post,* June 14, 1996.

Terry, Janice J. *U.S. Foreign Policy in the Middle East: The Role of Lobbies and Special Interest Groups*. London: Pluto, 2005.

Tetlock, Philip E. *Expert Political Judgment: How Good Is It? How Can We Know?* Princeton, NJ: Princeton University Press, 2005.

———. "How Accurate Are Your Pet Pundits?" Project Syndicate/Institute for Human Sciences, 2006. http://www.project-syndicate.org/commentary/tetlock1.

Thompson, Marilyn W. "Ex-Congressmen Lobby Hard on Turkey's Behalf." *International Herald Tribune,* October 17, 2007. http://www.iht.com/articles/2007/10/17/asia/lobby.php.

Thomson, James C., Jr. "How Could Vietnam Happen? An Autopsy." In *The Domestic Sources of American Foreign Policy: Insights and Evidence* (3rd ed.), ed. Eugene R. Wittkopf and James M. McCormick. Lanham, MD: Rowman & Littlefield, 1999.

"Through the Realist Lens: Conversation with John Mearsheimer." Conversations with History, Institute of International Studies, University of California, Berkeley, April 8, 2002. http://globetrotter.berkeley.edu/people2/Mearsheimer/mearsheimer-con0.html.

"Timeline: April 16, 1897: T. Roosevelt Appointed Assistant Secretary of the Navy." In *Crucible of Empire: The Spanish-American War*. PBS.org, 1999. http://www.pbs.org/crucible/tl7.html.

Tivnan, Edward. *The Lobby: Jewish Political Power and American Foreign Policy*. New York: Simon & Schuster, 1987.

"To the People of New York." Federalist Paper no. 10. November 23, 1787. http://www.yale.edu/lawweb/avalon/federal/fed10.htm.

Torchia, Christopher. "Turkey Threatens Repercussions for US." Associated Press, October 12, 2007.

Trask, David. *The War with Spain in 1898*. New York: Macmillan, 1981.

Trubowitz, Peter. *Defining the National Interest: Conflict and Change in American Foreign Policy*. Chicago: University of Chicago Press, 1998.

Urofsky, Melvin. *American Zionism from Herzl to the Holocaust.* Lincoln: University of Nebraska Press, 1995.

"U.S., Philippines, Hawaii, Latin America, in the 1920s." In *Macrohistory and World Report.* n.d. http://www.fsmitha.com/h2/ch14us.htm.

U.S. Department of State. "Remarks by the President on Cuba Policy." News release, October 24, 2007. http://www.state.gov/p/wha/rls/rm/07/q4/93965.htm.

Van Atta, John R. "Western Lands and the Political Economy of Henry Clay's American System, 1819–1832." *Journal of the Early Republic* 21, no. 4 (Winter 2001): 633–65.

Vanderbush, Walt, and Patrick J. Haney. "Policy toward Cuba in the Clinton Administration." *Political Science Quarterly* 114, no. 3 (Fall 1999): 387–408.

Waltz, Kenneth. *Theory of International Relations.* New York: McGraw-Hill, 1979.

"The War Party." *Panorama,* BBC, May 18, 2003. Available at http://news.bbc.co.uk/nol/shared/spl/hi/programmes/panorama/transcripts/thewarparty.txt.

"Washington's Farewell Address, 1796." http://www.yale.edu/lawweb/avalon/washing.htm.

Weinberg, Albert K. *Manifest Destiny.* Chicago: Quadrangle, 1963.

Werking, Richard H. "Senator Henry Cabot Lodge and the Philippines: A Note on American Territorial Expansion." *Pacific Historical Review* 42, no. 2 (May 1973): 234–40.

White House. "Remarks by the President in Recognition of Cuba Independence Day." News release, May 18, 2001. http://www.whitehouse.gov/news/releases/2001/05/20010518-7.html.

———. "President Bush Delivers Graduation Speech at West Point." News release, June 1, 2002. http://www.whitehouse.gov/news/releases/2002/06/20020601-3.html.

———. "President Delivers State of the Union Address." News release, January 29, 2002. http://www.whitehouse.gov/news/releases/2002/01/20020129-11.html.

———. "President Bush Discusses Top Priorities for the U.S." Press conference, July 30, 2003. http://www.whitehouse.gov/news/releases/2003/07/20030730-1.html.

Williams, William Appleman. *The Tragedy of American Diplomacy.* New York: Dell, 1962.

Willingham, Daniel T. "Critical Thinking: Why Is It So Hard to Teach?" *American Educator,* Summer 2007, 8–19.

Wittkopf, Eugene R., and James M. McCormick. "The Domestic Sources of American Foreign Policy." In *The Domestic Sources of American Foreign Policy: Insights and Evidence* (3rd ed.), ed. Eugene R. Wittkopf and James M. McCormick. New York: Rowman & Littlefield, 1999.

————, eds. *The Domestic Sources of American Foreign Policy: Insights and Evidence.* 3rd ed. New York: Rowman & Littlefield, 1999.

Wright, Thomas. "America's Neoconservatives—All Muscle, No History?" *Globalist,* September 15, 2004. http://www.theglobalist.com/DBWeb/StoryId.aspx?StoryId=4153.

Yglesias, Matthew. "Neoconservative Idealism." *Atlantic,* August 24, 2007. http://matthewyglesias.theatlantic.com/archives/2007/08/neoconservative_idealism.php.

Zakaria, Fareed. "The Politics of Rage: Why Do They Hate Us?" *Newsweek,* October 15, 2001, 22–40.

Zakaria, Tabassum, and Susan Cornwell. "House Panel OKs Armenian Genocide Resolution." Reuters, October 10, 2007. http://www.reuters.com/article/topNews/idUSWAT00825320071010.

Zinn, Howard. *A People's History of the United States.* New York: HarperCollins, 1995.

Index

abolitionists, 35
Abram, Morris B., 121
Abrams, Elliott, 67, 68, 90
adequate content knowledge, 11
Aguinaldo, Emilio, 47
AIPAC. *See* American Israel Public Affairs Committee
airborne warning and command system (AWACS), 116–17
Akins, Edwin F., 42
Alterman, Eric, 16–17
America Alone (Halper & Clarke), 136, 137–38
American Council for Judaism, 104
American Diplomacy (Kennan), 129
American Enterprise Institute, 64
American exceptionalism, 67, 138
American Foreign Policy (Hastedt), 28
American Friends of Vietnam (AFV), 55–59, 71, 154n6
American Hellenic Educational Progressive Association, 61
American Hellenic Institute, 61
American Israel Public Affairs Committee (AIPAC)
  Arab embargo of Israel and, 116
  emigration of Soviet Jews and, 114–15
  espionage charges against, 159n46
  founding and early history of, 111–12

influence over American policymaking, 112–14, 123
  as a model for CANF, 77
  monopolization of information about Israel, 114
  Presidents' Conference and, 117–18
  pushes Likud Party line, 160n56
  the Reagan administration and, 120
  relationship to the Israeli government, 118, 120, 121, 122
  suppression of free speech by Jews, 118
  U.S. Congress and, 159n37
  See also Israel lobby
American Jewish Committee, 99, 101, 104
American Jewish Congress, 101
American Jews
  collective feeling of vulnerability, 97, 98, 101
  historical overview, 97–102
  localism and, 121, 122–23
  postwar situation, 108–11
  Six Day War and its consequences, 109–11
  suppression of free speech for, 117–23
  Zionists, 100, 102–3
American Zionist Committee for Public Affairs, 111, 112–13

175